The Royle Family
My Arse

The best bits

The Royle Family
My Arse

The best bits

GRANADA

First published in Great Britain in 2001
By Granada Media, an imprint of André Deutsch Limited
20 Mortimer Street
London W1V 5HA

In association with Granada Media Group
Text copyright © Granada Media Group Ltd 2001
The Royle Family is a Granada Media Production

A catalogue record for this book is available from
the British Library.

Paperback ISBN 0 233 99996 5
Hardback ISBN 0 233 05027 2

Managing Art Director: Jeremy Southgate
Project Editor: Gillian Holmes
Design by Jill Bennett and Tony Woodruffe

Printed and bound in Italy
10 9 8 7 6 5 4 3 2 1

Photographs reproduced courtesy of Granada Media,
except for Series 3 photographs, © BBC

contents

introduction

The inspiration for The Royle Family came
from Caroline Aherne's frustration with TV
sitcoms. She wanted to write a show about
real people. As she said in an interview
'Nothing much happens, it's just a slice of
life'. Ironically, Caroline's success in
achieving her aim was confirmed in a
scornful review from The Socialist Worker
of all papers, who said 'Why would anyone
want to spend half an hour watching the
idiosyncrasies of a family on television,
when probably we all know similar families
to the Royles who we can visit?'

Well, quite a few people actually. The Royle
Family has become one of the best-loved
comedies on TV. And who can be surprised?
With a faultless cast and brilliant script,
even the most banal sentences become witty
one-liners.

That is why we have decided to put together
a book of the 'Best Bits'. It has proved an
almost impossible task as each episode just
got better and better. However, here is a
collection of scenes and lines that have
captured our imagination.

Everyone has their own favourite lines and we
hope you find yours in here.

Does my hair look like shite?

SERIES ONE

The Royle Wedding

SERIES ONE - THE CAST

Denise Royle		Caroline Aherne
Dave Best		Craig Cash
Twiggy		Geoffrey Hughes
Barbara Royle	(Mam)	Sue Johnston
Mary Carroll		Doreen Keogh
Antony Royle		Ralph Little
Joe Carroll		Peter Martin
Norma Speakman	(Nana)	Liz Smith
Cheryl Carroll		Jessica Stevenson
Jim Royle	(Dad)	Ricky Tomlinson

Episode 1

TEA-TIME – LIVING ROOM. DAD, MAM, DENISE.

IT'S HALF-PAST-SIX ON A FEBRUARY FRIDAY EVENING. A 26-YEAR-OLD WORKING-CLASS GIRL, DENISE ROYLE, IS SITTING WATCHING TV WITH HER MAM. HER DAD, JIM ROYLE IS SITTING READING A PHONE BILL. MAM AND DENISE SMOKE CONTINUOUSLY THROUGHOUT

DAD: **Ninety-eight quid...**

READING PHONE BILL

929 1246, whose number's that?

MAM: **It's Mary.**

it's good to talk my arse...

DAD: Mary!

You've been ringing Mary next door? if you shouted you could bloody hear her.

DENISE: She can hear you.

MAM: Give it a rest the pair of you.

DAD: Rest my arse... two pound fifty phoning next door... she's in and out all day like a bloody **yoyo.** PAUSE
I'll put you a serving hatch in.

DENISE: You're tight as a crab's arse you.

DAD: Crab's arse my arse. Two pound fifty...
good job she's cured her stutter.

NIGHT – LIVING ROOM. DAVE, DENISE, CHERYL TWIGGY, ANTONY, DAD, MAM

DAVE ENTERS, FOLLOWED BY DENISE AND CHERYL WITH GREETINGS FOR TWIGGY. TWIGGY IS A LARGE SCALLY BLOKE

ANTONY: It's all right, it's only Twiggy

DAD: TO KITCHEN Eh, **Twiggy's here**.

MAM: Hiya Twiggy, all right? TO TWIGGY **How's your mam's legs love?**

TWIGGY: Still under the hospital.

MAM: Tell her I was asking for her.

ALL: Hiya Twiggy

TWIGGY: Right... Now. How you fixed for denim... feel the quality of that.

DAD: **You've not got any wedding dresses in there?**

TWIGGY: No... these are jeans.

DENISE: What make are they?

TWIGGY: **Top gear... quality stuff... tenner a pair.**

CHERYL: **Got owt for me?**

ANTONY: Yeh... the ones he's wearing.

MAM: Eh Jim, why don't you get a pair? Them pants have gone at the crotch.

DAD: Don't look then.

DENISE: **Go on Dad, try some on.**

DAD: I don't wear jeans.

DAVE: Go on, Jim... everybody wears them nowadays.

TWIGGY: Come on... pants'll cost you three times the price of these and these'll last you twice as long. Try them on.

DAD: Give us a pair here. HE EXITS

TWIGGY: What about you, Denise?

DENISE: **I've not got the arse for jeans.**

TWIGGY: **You have, you've got a gorgeous arse you have... you'll find these out a treat.**

DAVE: **Hey!** That's my fiancée's arse you're talking about.

TWIGGY: Yeh... and that's your arse you're talking through. TO MAM
I'll tell you what, I've got a load of Wash'n'Go, I don't know whether you're interested.

MAM: What've you got?

TWIGGY: Wash'n'Go, y'know the stuff that bird in the ad washes with an' pisses off. It's the genuine stuff but with Arabic writing on it. **50p a bottle.**

NO RESPONSE FROM OTHERS

Please yourself.

CHERYL: Go on then Twiggy, I'll have two quid's worth.

TWIGGY: Tell you what... for you luv, cos you're my best-looking customer... I'll throw in a box of panty pads. Now how are you for jeans Cheryl?

CHERYL: I'm on a diet. I don't really know what size to get.

TWIGGY: **Well... if they're too tight I'll help you out of 'em.**

NUDGING MAM. BOTH LAUGH

MAM: Uh Twiggy, you're a right cheeky beggar. Ahh, how's little Lee?

TWIGGY: She lets me see him every other Saturday and every third Wednesday from four till seven.

MAM: He must be getting big now.

TWIGGY: Yeh, he's twelve in August. I'll tell you what, he's a fussy little bleeder... it's got to be Nike this and Levi that... he won't touch any of this shite. So what you doing Cheryl... are you having a pair or what?

CHERYL: No. I don't think so.

DAD RETURNS WITH JEANS. ALL LAUGH EXCEPT DAD.

DAD: **All right you shower of shite.**

DAVE: **Hey it's John Wayne.**

TWIGGY: Here give em back... you'll give me a bad name.

DAD: Laugh all you want, I'm keeping these. My money's in my other trousers. I owe you a tenner, Twiggy. It's like ruddy Blackpool illuminations in here... turn that lamp off. Turn that fire off an' all. If you're cold get a vest on.
Where's the remote Barbara?

CUT

Episode 2

 TEA-TIME – LIVING ROOM. DAD, DENISE, MAM, ANTONY ARE EATING AT THE TABLE

MAM: Mary next door's got a microwave.

DENISE: Me and Dave's going to have a microwave... do you think I should get a food processor.

DAD: What for? **Just stick to the chip pan love.**

DENISE: **We're not going to have chips every night.**

MAM: **What are you going to have then?**

DENISE: **I don't know, we might have pasta and stuff like that.**

DAD: **Pasta my arse.**

MAM: **Have you told Dave this?**

DENISE: **Yeh.**

DAD: **And he still wants to marry you?**

DENISE: He's not marrying me for what I'm like in the kitchen.

ANTONY: It's what you're like in the bedroom.

DAD: Hey, cut it out.

DENISE: TO ANTONY Who threw you nuts? TO MAM What I'm going to do is... I'm going to make lasagne and I'm going to stick it in the freezer so he can heat it up when he gets home.

MAM: Look at you Denise... you've got it all mapped out. I wish I was like you.

You know, when I was your age we knew nothing.

CUT

MAM, DENISE, DAD, ANTONY SITTING ROUND THE TABLE AFTER TEA

MAM: TO DENISE **Oh your nana's coming for the day, Sunday.**

DENISE: Who's going to pick her up?

MAM: Your dad can go and get her on the bus.

DAD: Why can't she get the bus on her own?

MAM: # She's eighty-two.

DAD: ## She should know the way then.

MAM: You're going.

DAD: She manages to get the bus to bingo every week.

MAM: ### You'd go if it was your mother.

DAD: ### I'd have a job, she's been dead fifteen years.

MAM: Ah. She'll be looking forward to coming all week.

ANTONY: All she does when she comes here is watch telly.

MAM: Well it's nice for her to watch telly in someone else's house. It's company for her.

DAD: ### If I get like that, shoot me.

ANTONY: # Who's got a gun?

LIVING ROOM. ANTONY, DAD, MAM, DENISE, DAVE

ANTONY: AT WINDOW **Hey look**, Jacko's got a new motor.

DENISE: COMING TO WINDOW **Oh 'ere y'are**, here's Lorraine coming out to look at it. She never has them leggin's off her. Mam come and look at Lorraine looking at Jacko's car in her leggings.

MAM: COMING TO WINDOW She never wears nowt but them leggings, her.

DAD: STILL SITTING **That's how come they can afford a new car.**

MAM: Oh, look at Carol over the road gawping through the window. You'd think she'd never seen a car before.

DENISE: # She's not going to drive it in her slippers is she?

DAVE: **He's not going to let her drive that, she's always bladdered.**

DENISE: How much more can you look at a car? Look at her getting the manual out... as if she knows what she's looking at.

DAD: FROM CHAIR **What sort of car is it Antony?**

ANTONY: # Sierra.

DAD: **What an estate?**

ANTONY: **No saloon.**

DAD: Is it a hatchback?

ANTONY: Come and look yourself.

DAD: # You're a lazy little sod you.

MAM: # It's a red one, Jim.

DAD: What's the bodywork like?

MAM: I've just told you, it's red.

DAD: Thank you, Jeremy Clarkson.

DAD REMAINS SEATED WATCHING TELLY CUT

Episode 3

 AFTERNOON – KITCHEN. DAVE, ANTONY AND JIM. THERE IS A KNOCK AT THE DOOR.

DAD: OPENS DOOR **All right Joe, you busy?**

JOE: **No.**

DAD: **Right... Are you having a brew?**

JOE: **No, I won't thanks.**

DAD: **Do you want a damaged cake?**

JOE: AFTER A BIT OF THOUGHT **Aye, go on then.**

DAD: **Do you go up the Pear Tree, Joe?**

JOE: **No.** PAUSE **I don't like the bitter.**

DAVE: **Neither does my bumhole, it's like a chewed orange.**

DAD: STRUGGLING FOR CONVERSATION **Antiques Roadshow's on in a minute.**

JOE: # Oh aye?

DAD: Barbara's mother's down, why don't you nip through and say hello.

JOE: No.

PAUSE

DAD: ## So life treating you all right is it?

JOE: Can't complain. PAUSE Nice bit of cake.

DAVE: Did you hear the thunder last night?

JOE: No.

DAVE: Slept right through it then?

JOE: Must have done.

DAD: Antony, nip through and see if we can go in.

MARY ENTERS

MARY: YOU'RE ALL RIGHT TO GO IN NOW. OH DAVE, YOU'RE IN FOR A TREAT. TO JOE ARE YOU STOPPING JOE?

JOE: No.

MARY AND JOE EXIT

DAD: ## Bloody hell, he's hard work ain't he?

DAVE: # I wonder if he'd give me any tips for my wedding speech.

CUT

LIVING ROOM. DAVE, DENISE, NANA, MAM, DAD. DAVE IS EATING A CRUNCHIE

DAVE: UNWRAPPING CRUNCHIE Are you sure you didn't want any Denise?

DENISE: Eat it quick before I change my mind.

DAVE: EATING SLOWLY Hmm, lovely chocolate... hmmm, honeycomb centre.

DENISE: # Ah, don't be tight, Dave.

DAVE: OVERACTING **Hmmm,**
          it's the best chocolate bar I've had... **ever**.

NANA: 'Tis nice, in't it.

DENISE: Nana! TO DAVE Just give us the end of it then.

DAVE: No... I'm thinking of you.

DENISE: No, come on now, I'm not messing.

DAVE: No, I'm not taking Bella Emberg down the aisle. RELENTING
          Here y'are.

DENISE: ## No... I don't want it now.

          DAVE HOLDS IT UP TO HIS MOUTH IN SLOW MOTION, TEASING AS IF HE'S GOING TO EAT IT

          There's something wrong with you.

          DAVE EATS THE LAST BIT

          ## You ate it! Cheers... I'm not marrying you now.

DAVE: **And I'm bothered!**

MAM: That's not a reason not to marry him.

DENISE: I'm only joking.

NANA: He'll be back to that Beverley if you're not careful.

CUT

Episode 4

 LIVING ROOM. DAD, MAM, DENISE, ANTONY, DAVE, CHERYL.

DAD'S BIRTHDAY. THERE ARE FIVE BIRTHDAY CARDS UP. DENISE IS LYING ON THE SOFA. DAD SITS WATCHING TV. MAM ENTERS WITH A GLASS OF WATER AND TWO TABLETS.

MAM: **Here you are, luv.**
OFFERING DENISE TABLETS AND WATER **How do you feel now?**

DENISE: I'll tell you where it is... it's behind that eye and behind that eye, across there... it won't let up.

MAM: **I think it's stress related.**

DAD: Funny how you always get stress after you've had seventeen halves of lager.

MAM: **Ahh, show us that card you got off my mam.**

DAD: It's on the mantelpiece.

MAM: ## Pass it to us, Jim.

DAD: PASSING CARD – WITH GOLFER ON THE FRONT – TO MAM **Twenty-five years she's known me. How many times has she seen me playing golf?**

MAM: It's the sentiment in't it? READS **Happy Birthday Jim... love Norma.**

DAD: She's hardly gone overboard on the sentiment.

Barbara Cartland's job's safe.

MAM: Was there a fiver in it?

DAD: Yeh... same one as I'll be giving her back next month on her birthday. It's a bloody swizz this birthday lark.

DENISE: Ah Dad, did you like them socks?

DAD: Yeh.

DENISE: I didn't know whether to get you them or a BMW.

DAD: ## You did right luv.

LIVING ROOM, DAD, DENISE, DAVE, ANTONY, MAM, MARY, JOE CELEBRATING JIM'S BIRTHDAY.

MAM: **How's your Kit Kat Joe?**

JOE: Nice.

MAM: How about the lager?

JOE: **Nice.**

MARY: Will you be celebrating in the Feathers tonight?

DAD: **Oh aye... it's non-stop.**

Are you going for a jar, Joe?

JOE: What time will you be in?

DAD: **All night.**

JOE: **No.**

LIVING ROOM. MAM HAS BEEN TRYING UNSUCCESSFULLY TO TAKE A PHOTO OF DAD, DENISE, DAVID, ANTONY, MARY, JOE

MARY: Let me take one of just the family.

MARY AND MAM CHANGE PLACES BUT JOE STILL STANDS IN PICTURE.

MARY: # Say cheese.

ALL: HALF-HEARTEDLY Cheese.

MARY: I can't turn it on.

MAM: RESCUING THE CAMERA It's the end of the film, Mary.

MARY: I think I've clicked twice on that last one.

DAD: Is it twenty-four or a thirty-six?

MAM: I don't know.

DAD: Well what number is it on?

MAM: I don't know, it's rewound.

MARY: It's a nice camera that, Barbara.

MAM: It's from Argos... we got that for...
what did we get that for, Jim?

DAD: # For taking bloody photographs.

LIVING ROOM. DAD, DAVE, DENISE, MAM, ANTONY

DAD: TO DAVE **How's work then, lad?**

DAVE: **I had a job in Blakely this morning... four flights of stairs for some shitty old wardrobe and a chest of drawers.**

DAD: **That's what you're paid for in't it?**

DAVE: **Yeh, but you want a bit of job satisfaction don't you?**

DAD: **Did you get a tip?**

DAVE: **She gave us a bathroom cabinet. I had to unscrew it from the wall though.**

DENISE: **We're not having any shitey second-hand stuff... I'm having everything new from Ikea.**

DAVE: **In your dreams. I can't afford them sort of prices.**

DAD: **I bet you get a load of tips don't you?**

DAVE: **I get the odd fiver. It's the rich ones that are the tightest... it's the poor dears that haven't got two ha'pennies to rub together that want to drop you a couple of quid.**

DAD: **And you take it!**

DAVE: **Dead right. I'll give you a tip, Jim always have a big top pocket and when your hands are full they can drop it in there. Oh aye, you've got to be on the ball in this game.**

DAD, DENISE, CHERYL, MAM, DAVE, ANTONY ARE READING HOROSCOPES

MAM: Is that Russell Grant?... He's very good.

DAD: # He's as camp as Christmas.

DENISE: What if he is?

DAD: He's someone to talk about Uranus.

DAVE, DAD AND ANTONY LAUGH.

DENISE: ## I'll tell you who else is gay.

DAVE: ## Who?

DENISE: ## Antony.

ANTONY: Get real.

DAVE: ## Richard Gere's gay.

DENISE: No way.

DAVE: I'm telling you, it's common knowledge down the Feathers.

DAD: Oh right... you mean that showbiz Mecca... they've got a direct line to Hollywood in the bar.

MAM: He's married to Cindy Crawford.

DAVE: No he split up over...

DENISE: Over what?

DAVE: ## Over Easter.

DENISE: No, what did they split up over?

DAVE: Cos he's a fruit, in't he?

MAM: MISSING THE POINT **And he's now with Russell Grant is he?**

DAD: DOING UP HIS COLLAR **So... Cindy Crawford's free is she?**

MAM: I don't care what anybody is... whether they're gay, straight, Australian. It's what they're like as a person that counts.

DAD: Steady on Barbara, It's not Live Aid it's my birthday.

Episode 5

LIVING ROOM – NIGHT. DENISE AND DAVE ARE ARGUING

DENISE: UPSET **If you think I'll marry you now, you pig. I'm not.**
A load of lads fancy me but I never bother with them.

DAVE: Well bother with them if you want to.

DENISE: I don't want to. Every time we see Beverley Macca it's the same.
You love flirting with her. I saw your face, you love it.

DAVE: **I'm not even talking about this crap.**

DENISE: I could wear a low top like that and a bleeding mini-skirt but I've got
more respect for myself, but you don't, you don't respect me.

MAM ENTERS AND COMFORTS DENISE WHO IS NOW IN TEARS

MAM: **Dave, what have you done now?**

DAVE: **I've done nowt.**

MAM: Well she's not crying over nothing is she?

DENISE: He was flirting with Beverley Macca.

DAVE: **Was I hell... I'm a DJ, right... she was asking for a record.**

DENISE: Yeh, 'All right, darling' he kept saying to her. Why did you give her a kiss when she went?

DAVE: She came over to me.

DENISE: GETTING EMOTIONAL **Every time I came out of the toilet she was round hi** like flies around shit and TO DAVE **you're the shit and she's not even th** **fly cos she's too fat to be a fly, she's the shit as well, that's what you** **are, two shovels of shit... and that's it.**

MAM: We don't have to bring shit into it.

LIVING ROOM. DAD, MAM, DENISE. THE ARGUMENT IS CALMING DOWN. DAD HAD MADE DRINKS FOR EVERYONE

DAD IS PICKING HIS NOSE

DENISE: **Dad, stop picking your nose.**

DAD: How can you be bothered about me picking my nose with all the troubles you've got.

MAM: **Haven't you got a hanky?**

DAD: What in my pyjamas?

There's barely enough room for my tackle.

MAM: Do we need to know, Jim?

DAD: Is that it, kiddo? Is it all off then?

DENISE: I don't know I've got to have a think in my head.

MAM: Do you remember when Dave first came round? He never said a word for three months then he took that old armchair to the tip for us and it really broke the ice.

DAD: # Bloody hell, you don't half talk some rubbish, Barbara.

MAM: ## Well it did.

DAD: Well, he's better than that Stuart lad you went out with from the flats... he was a gormless get him. He couldn't find his arse with both hands.

MAM: Uh, I was happy when you broke that engagement off. PAUSE Do you remember when Dave came to Cleethorpes with us in that four-berth and he took his shoes off and nobody dared say owt?

DAD: I bloody did, they were rife. They wanted a stake through them.

DENISE: They've gone a lot better now I've got him that stuff from the Avon.

MAM: ## You see, he does make an effort for you.

LIVING ROOM. DENISE, DAD, MAM, DAVE.
ANTONY ENTERS WITH TEA

DAD: **Hey flash, forget the tea, just bring the whisky.**

MAM: Look at him now, I'm glad I didn't call the doctor.

DENISE: Ey Dave, do my dad that **impression of Paul Daniels** you do.

DAVE: No, go 'way.

DENISE: Go on.

MAM: # Go on Dave, I love impressions.

DAVE: No.

MAM: No go on.

ANTONY: Who's he doing?

DAVE: That's magic.

ONLY DENISE LAUGHS

ANTONY: That's Orville.

DAD: # Rory Bremner's job's safe isn't it.

DAVE: Hey, remember that time they had Paul Daniels on Spitting Image in bed with Debbie. He was balancing a glass of milk on his head and he whipped his rug off from under it and the milk stays on his head... LAUGH **THAT WAS TOP THAT.**

DAVE AND DENISE LAUGH

DAD: You're a bit simple you two.

MAM: Is that that thing with puppets? I never got that me.
I don't like puppets me.

DAD: You like the Muppets.

MAM: Yes, I like the Muppets.

Lig

Episode 6

DENISE'S BEDROOM. DENISE, CHERYL, MAM

DENISE: Now look at me. Come 'ere be honest – is that too much blusher?

MAM: **You can't have too much blusher on your wedding day.**

CHERYL: Well, you're the blushing bride aren't you? LAUGHS

s a fag, Cheryl.

KITCHEN. DAVE, DAD, TWIGGY

NANA: Where's your best man? Barry is it?

DAVE: **No Gary... he's got to work.** He couldn't get the morning off. **He's going straight from the butchers.**

DAD: That's all we want, church stinking of bloody mince.

TWIGGY: Hey, watch what will happen...he'll put his hand in his pocket for the ring and **pull out a pork chop!** LAUGHS

CUT TO:

BEDROOM. DENISE, MAM, CHERYL, NANA

DENISE: CRYING I hate my hair, he's downstairs, it's all going wrong.

MAM: Never mind, luv... it's all too much in't it.

DENISE: **What's he doing down there?**

CHERYL: He's just with your dad and Twiggy. He says his arse is like that.

DENISE/
MAM: # Ah!

CHERYL: **Uh yeh, gorgeous...** Ey, I think Twiggy's trying to cop with me.

DENISE: You wouldn't go with him, would you?

CHERYL: ## No... Twiggy! No way.

DENISE: You would, wouldn't you.

CHERYL: # Yeh, I would.

*Mr and Mrs Jim Royle
cordially invite you to
the wedding of their daughter
Denise Royle to Dave Best*

*The ceremony will commence at
11am on May 19, at St. Peter's Church,
with a reception afterwards
at the Feathers public house.*

*Entertainment will be provided
courtesy of Dave's mobile disco
followed by live music from Exit.*

*The wedding list is at Argos.
Please quote reference: Royle wedding.*

R S V P

BEDROOM. NANA, DENISE, CHERYL, TWIGGY

TWIGGY KNOCKS ON THE BEDROOM DOOR. DENISE IS NOW MADE-UP BUT IS STILL IN HER DRESSING GOWN

TWIGGY: Hey Norma, no sliding down the banister, girl. Are you decent?

DENISE: Yeh.

TWIGGY: Ah, I'll come in anyway. LAUGHS Hey Denise, you look lovely,

DENISE: **It's only my dressing gown.**

TWIGGY: I know but if you look that good in a dressing gown... Hey this is your last chance... I've got a fast car downstairs... two tickets to Rio in the glovebox and a load of knock-off sports gear in the boot... what do you say?

DENISE: **Ah, you're tempting me now, Twiggy.**

CHERYL: What sort of sports gear you got?

TWIGGY: Well I've got a load of tracky bottoms, I'm getting them out at the reception. I'll sort you out.

DENISE: **Hey, how's Dave?**

TWIGGY: I'm not sure that he isn't having second thoughts but he's got a lovely suit on but he's wearing pair of running shoes.

DENISE: Don't Twiggy, I'm a bag of nerves. Imagine what a state I'd look if he didn't turn up.

TWIGGY: Hey, but imagine what a state he'd look when you'd caught him. He's skipping off nowhere. I'll break his legs for you if I have to.

DENISE: **Ah, cheers Twiggy.**

TWIGGY EXITS

DENISE: Heart of gold him in't it?

CHERYL: **To be honest if there's no one better... I'm going to cop with him tonight.**

DENISE: **Ah... he'd be made up with that.**

 SITTING ROOM. MARY, JOE, DAD, MAM, NANA, ANTONY

DAD: POURING DRINK Barbara?

MAM: Just a little one, luv.

DAD: Norma?

NANA: Yes please.

ANTONY: Can I have one Dad?

DAD: No.

MARY: Oh, look at Antony's lovely haircut. You look like a little choirboy.

DAD: **He looks like a little gay boy.**

MAM: You know, I've been so busy this morning I've hardly smoked.
TO DAD Give us one now.

CHERYL ENTERS

CHERYL: Are you ready? ... Here comes the bride.

DAD LEADS EVERYONE TO SING THE TUNE OF 'HERE COMES THE BRIDE'. DENISE ENTERS. SHE'S NOW GOT HER VEIL ON AND CARRIES A DOLLY BAG. LOTS OF 'AHHS'.

MARY: Isn't she lovely!

DENISE: # Does my hair look like shite?

Mary: No, you look gorgeous. Oh Jim, you must be so proud. Oh, look at the pair of you... Denise the blushing b ride, our Cheryl in dusky peach.

ANTHONY: Eh Denise, you look dead nice in that dress, honest.

DENISE: Cheers Ant... you don't look too bad yourself.

NANA: Them earrings set it off a treat, Denise.

DENISE: Thanks Nana.

NANA: **Don't lose them.**

DAD: 'An't she got enough to worry about?

DENISE: # Dad, giz a ciggie... calm my nerves.

DAD: Take your time.

JOE: Denise.

DENISE: Hiya Joe.

JOE: **Nice outfit.**

DENISE: Thanks Joe.

DAD: **Steady on Joe... you silver-tongued charmer.**

DENISE: It's me last day here.

Will you miss us, Ant?

ANTONY: Yeh, like a hole in a parachute. I'm having your room.

DENISE: Get lost, that's my room. What if me and Dave want to stop over?

ANTONY: You only live round the corner.

DENISE: **Mam, tell 'em.**

LIVING ROOM.
EVERYONE'S LEFT EXCEPT DAD AND DENISE.

DAD: Ey, come and see your nana. Bloody hell, who else would get in a taxi arse first like that?

DENISE COMES OVER AND LOOKS OUT OF THE WINDOW

DAD: Y'mam looks good, doesn't she... she's done you proud there... and Antony, he scrubbed up all right. **What's up cock?**

DENISE: WELLING UP **Nothing...** it's just the last time I'll be Denise Royle... it's dead weird getting married... I just hope I like it.

DAD: Ahh Denise, you'll love it. Do you know, you look radiant. **You look like a little princess. I'm dead proud of you.**

DENISE: **Even though I never kept down a job?**

DAD: That doesn't matter now, luv... Let the other silly bugger do it...

DOORBELL RINGS.

DAD: (LOOKING OUT OF THE WINDOW) Ey, look at that car... shame we're only going as far as the church in it.

DAD GOES TO THE FRONT DOOR

DENISE: **Tell them I'm not ready yet.** DENISE WIPES HER EYES

DAD: (OOV) SHOUTING TO DRIVER **Won't be a minute, pal, just a few last-minute preparations.** COMING BACK IN **Preparations my arse.** POURING WHISKY **Let's have a drop of whisky.** PASSING CIGARETTE
Ey kid... have a ciggie off your old dad.

DENISE LIGHTS UP

She does look a sight in that bridesmaid dress, doesn't she, Cheryl. JOKING **Mind you, makes you look a damn- sight better in the photos.**

DENISE: Dad! Y'know, Dad,
I never say anything nice to you
I'm always going on at you for p
your nose and farting...

DAD: **I know luv...**

DENISE: **You and m'mam... more than anything.**

DAD: **I know. Here kid.** OFFERING TOAST **To you!**

BOTH CLICK GLASSES AND DOWN THE DRINK IN ONE.

DAD: LEAVING **Uhh, I hope my arse holds up.**

DAD EXITS. DENISE HESITATES AND LOOKS BACK AT ROOM, THEN EXITS

I really want Keanu,
but Dave wants Dave.

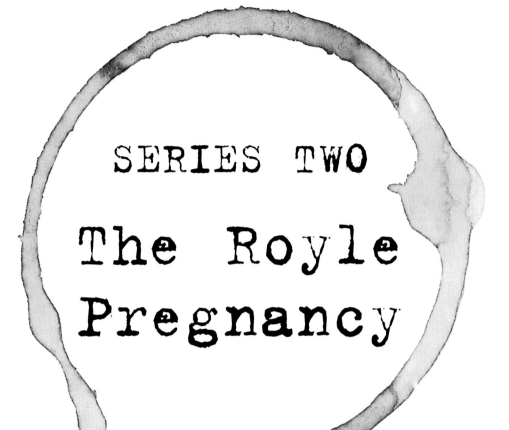

SERIES TWO

The Royle Pregnancy

Learning
to be a
mum

SERIES TWO — THE CAST

Denise Royle		Caroline Aherne
Dave Best		Craig Cash
Twiggy		Geoffrey Hughes
Barbara Royle	(Mam)	Sue Johnston
Mary Carroll		Doreen Keogh
Antony Royle		Ralph Little
Joe Carroll		Peter Martin
Norma Speakman	(Nana)	Liz Smith
Emma		Sheridan Smith
Cheryl Carroll		Jessica Stevenson
Jim Royle	(Dad)	Ricky Tomlinson
Darren		Andrew Whyment

Episode 1

 LIVING ROOM. BARBARA, ANTONY ALL WATCHING TV

MAM: **Don't it look lovely there.**

DAD: # Bermuda my arse,

MAM: She's looking her age though in't she, Judith Chalmers?

JIM LOOKS AT BARBARA. PAUSE.

MAM: She's got some lovely wrap-round skirts though. Who do you thinks the oldest, her or Gloria Hunniford, Jim? Jim?

DAD: What?

MAM: **Who do you think's the oldest, her or Gloria Hunniford?**

DAD: **I couldn't give a shiny shite. Bloody 'ell, Barb**

BARBARA SHAKES HER HEAD. PAUSE

ANTONY: **Eh, y'know Darren's cousin, Steve?**

MAM: Yeah.

ANTONY: **He's been abroad twice this year.**

MAM: Ooh.

DAD: Oh aye, where did he go lad?

ANTONY: Ah, he went to **Magaluf** in February and, eh, Lloret de Mar in July.

DAD: He's hardly Alan bloody Whicker is he? Na, them foreign holidays are a swizz. Them bloody travel agents ripping every bugger off and mugs like him fall for it.

MAM: **What are they falling for, Jim?**

DAD: Well, there's nothing you can do abroad that you can't do here. It just costs you twice as bloody much.

MAM: **They're on their holidays – they're having a good time.**

DAD: Having a good time, my arse. They spend half the time on the khazi, don't they, having the wild shites. You may as well do that here in the comfort of your own home.

MAM: **You're a miserable sod, Jim, you are.** 🎬 CUT

────────────────

 LIVING ROOM, SAME NIGHT.
DENISE AND DAVE HAVE ARRIVED.

MAM: Have you had your teas?

DENISE/
DAVE: **Yeah.**

PAUSE

MAM: What d'ya have?

DENISE: **Dairylea** on **toast**.

DAD: Bloody 'ell girl, Dairylea on toast. Come on now. Eh? Delia Smith's got nothing to worry about, has she.

DENISE: **I made it myself.**

DAD: **Go 'way.**

DAVE: I don't mind Dairylea me.

LIVING ROOM. SAME NIGHT. ANTONY HAS GONE TO THE KITCHEN TO MAKE BACON BUTTIES FOR EVERYONE

DENISE: **Dad.**

DAD: What?

Denise: **Your fly-hole's undone.**

DAD: ZIPPING IT UP **Ah, the cage might be open but the beast's asleep.**

MAM: **Beast my arse.**

CUT TO JIM'S FACE. PAUSE. ALL CONTINUE TO WATCH TELLY. PAUSE

DENISE: **Mam.**

MAM: **Ummm**

DENISE: Mam, can you ask our Antony to make my bacon dead, dead crispy.

MAM: Yeah, Antony, can you make Denise's bacon dead, dead crispy.

PAUSE, ALL WATCHING TV. BARBARA LIGHTS UP.

MAM: OFFERING CIGGY 'Ere y'are love.

DENISE: Oh, no thanks.

MAM: **Have you given up.**

DENISE: # Yeah.

MAM: You've always loved smoking.

DENISE: Yeah well, me and Dave's got something to tell ya.

DAVE: **You said you weren't gonna say owt.**

DENISE: Yeah, I know, well, I am now.

DAVE: **You said it was a big secret.**

DENISE: Yeah, but that was this morning. Mam, Dad, we're pregnant

MAM: **When did you find out?**

DENISE: Well, me period was late, right, JIM SHOOTS A LOOK OF DISDAIN and then I was really really sick, but I thought, oh, you know, it was just a hangover 'cause the night before we'd had a lock-in at the Feathers. But then the next day, I was really sick again so I went down to Boots, right, and got a pregnancy kit – ten quid they are – and, em anyway, the line came up in the square window.

MAM: REALLY EXCITED Oh, Denise – the square window.

DENISE: Yes. So I was shouting for Dave at the top of the stairs – but he was watching something on telly. What was you watching Dave?

DAVE: Never Mind the Buzzcocks.

DENISE: And, em, then he come up. And I'm like this: 'Hey Daddy, Daddy, guess what?', like that to him, didn't I, Dave?

DAVE: Ummm.

MAM: And did he know what you meant?

DENISE/
DAVE: TOGETHER **No, no.**

DENISE: But then I said, you know, 'Dave, I'm pregnant', like that and, er, the penny dropped, didn't it?

DAVE: **Yeah, straight away, yeah.**

DENISE: And eh, then I let him have a little look in the square window.

MAM: Ooh, the square window. Bet you were delighted weren't you, Dave?

DAVE: Oh yeah. Big style.

DAD: Ten quid for a bloody pregnancy test. Bloody highway robbery.

MAM: Antony bring me the phone. ANTONY GOES TO HALL TO GET PHONE **I'm gonna tell your nana.**

DENISE: **Aah. Mam, will you let me tell her?**

MAM: Oh, all right then. DIALS DELIGHTEDLY **Hiya, hiya, Mam. Mam, our Denise and Dave have got something very special to tell you.**
PAUSE **Oh, okay then. Bye.** PUTS PHONE DOWN **Can we ring her back after Corrie.**

CUT

LIVING ROOM. DAD, DENISE, DAVE, MAM.

MAM: Have you thought of any names yet?

DENISE: I've thought about nothing else, but everything I like, he doesn't like. If it's a girl, I really want Whitney.

MAM: Aah, Whitney. That's gorgeous. Whitney. What if it's a boy?

DENISE: Well, I really want Keanu, but Dave wants Dave.

MAM: I don't think you should have a Dave.

DENISE: No.

MAM: I mean, Dave's a Dave. What do you think, Jim?

DAD: Eh? What about?

MAM: Well, if it's a boy, Dave wants to call it Dave.

DAD: TO DAVE Well, you're already a Dave. What d'you want another one for? Come on, son, get a bloody grip of yourself.

DENISE: See.

DAVE: Well it's like handing it down, innit. I mean, my dad was Dave, and his dad, and I think his dad was as well. PAUSE And his dad.

DAD: Well it's about time you put a bloody stop to it. C'mon.

Episode 2

 LIVING ROOM. DAD, TWIGGY, NANA, ANTONY, DAVE, DENISE AND MAM.

MAM HAS BEEN COOKING DINNER. DAD AND TWIGGY HAVE BEEN TO THE PUB. TWIGGY, DAD, DENISE, DAVE, ANTONY, NANA ARE JUST SITTING DOWN TO EAT. MAM IS BRINGING IT IN.

TWIGGY: I'll go round there. Don't worry about me Barb. I'll eat any old shite.

DENISE: You'll have to come round to mine and Dave's one time for Sunday dinner.

DAD: Oh, nice one.

DENISE: Mam can cook there. Be a nice change for her.

DAVE: Ah, yeah.

NANA: That's too much for me, Barbara.

TWIGGY: It's all right, I'll polish off anything you can't eat.

NANA: Oh, this gravy looks watery, Barbara. I usually put cornflour in mine. You've never tasted my gravy, have you, Twiggy?

DENISE: Oh, ta.

TWIGGY: Can't say I've had the pleasure.

DAVE: **Hey, Bob the Spark was in the pub, Nana.**

NANA: **Ooh, what's to do with it?**

DAVE: He doesn't know, he's not had a chance to look at it yet.

NANA: **Ooh, I'm lost without it.**

DAD: You never bloody use it. We always have to record everything for ya.

NANA: Well I like watching Dave and Denise's wedding video on it. D'you know Elsie? Lives next door to me? She's seen it five times.

DAD: Well that must be bloody entertaining, watching a crowd of people you don't know.

NANA: Well she feels like she knows you all. It's company you know when you live on your own.

BARBARA SITS DOWN, HOT AND FLUSTERED

DAD: # All right, Barb?

MAM: Yes.

DAD: **You're as red as a bloody beetroot.**

MAM: It's nothing. Just leave it.

DENISE: Eh, Twiggy, who's this new ladyfriend what you've got then?

TWIGGY: Eh, she's a tasty piece – I think this could be the one.

ALL: Aah.

DAD: That's what the three lads said who have kids to her.

TWIGGY: Nothing wrong with that.

DAD: Nothing said.

MAM: Hey, Twiggy, you'll have to bring her round one night and introduce her to us.

TWIGGY: Yeah, I'd love to, but she works nights in a petrol station.

MAM: Oh, does she? Oh, that's a dangerous job in't it for young girl, working nights in a petrol station.

DAD: You haven't seen her, Barb. Lennox Lewis wouldn't tangle with her.

TWIGGY: Yeah, she's well capable of handling herself.

MAM: Aah.

DAD: Bloody 'ell, Barb, how long have these roasties been in?

 MAM, DAD, NANA, TWIGGY, DENISE, DAVE, ANTONY, STILL AT THE TABLE, CONVERSATION HAS TURNED TO RICHARD BRANSON

ANTONY: Hey, he's loaded, he is. He's worth over a billion.

DAD: Bloody 'ell that's only about ten quid less than you, isn't it, Nana?

DAVE: D'you know how he started off his business that Branson?
From a little record shop.

MAM: Ooh, can't imagine him behind a record shop can you? With his beard.

DAD: **What's his beard got to do with it?**

MAM: Ey, imagine what it must be like to be him. All that money.

DAD: Can't get that rich without being as tight as a camel's arse in a sandstorm, can ya? He wouldn't give you the steam off his piss that fella.

BARBARA AND TWIGGY LIGHT UP AT THE END OF THE MEAL

DENISE: **Mam, give us a little drag of that ciggy.**

DAVE: No.

DENISE: **I'm only asking for a little drag.**

DAVE: **No.**

DENISE: Oh, one little drag on a Sunday dinner's not gonna harm it.

DAVE: Course it is. Any smokin's bound to harm it.

DENISE: Oh, I'll tell you what, right Dave, I'll do everything for this baby.
I'll carry it on my own for nine months, no smoking, no drinking...

DAVE: **No drinking?**

DENISE: Yeah well. Hardly any. Yeah well, what about you? You can't even be arsed to move that moped out of the box-room to make it into a nursery. Will you tell him, Mam?

CUT

BACK ON THE SUBJECT OF THE BIKE...

TWIGGY: I'll tell you what, I'll pop round tomorrow, Dave, and give you a price for that.

DAVE: **I don't know about that, Twig.**

DENISE: I do. We're getting rid of that bike. Oh no, I'm putting my foot down. It's bad Feng Shui to have a bike in bits in your box-room.

DAD: **Feng Shui my arse**

MAM: **Good for you, Denise.**

ANTONY: You know what, I reckon you should keep that bike, Dave. Yeah, I do yeah.

DENISE: It's nothing to do with you, Antony.

Shut your big fat gob, you big fat pig.

Mam, will you tell him?

TWIGGY FINALLY LEAVES

ANTONY: **See ya, Twigg.**

DAVE: See ya, Twigg.

DAD: **Ta-da, pal.** One greedy scrounging get that fella, in't he. What a bloody brass neck, fancy coming back here for his Sunday dinner.

DAVE: You asked him, Jim.

DAD: I know, but I didn't think he'd say yes.

MAM: **Do you know, Jim!**
You've got more faces than the town hall clock.

Nana: **And every one of 'em's miserable.**

Episode 3

 LIVING ROOM. MAM AND DAD ARE WATCHING TELLY.

MAM: **Ooh.** Ainsley Harriott's bathroom. Oh Jim, put BBC on – it's Changing Rooms.

DAD: **I'm watching that.**

MAM: You're not, you're reading the paper.

DAD: Yes, I'm reading the paper, but I'm listening to that.

MAM: **No put Changing Rooms on.**

DAD: TUTS Bloody 'ell, what did your last slave die of? HE PRESSES THE REMOTE Bloody 'ell, if you call that entertainment, watching a Cockney knocking nails into plywood, I don't know, is that what it's coming to.

MAM: **Shut up, Jim.**

DAD: Hard to believe it. Look at him, the bloody old nancy-boy tie-dyeing the neighbour's bloody curtains... I'm glad we don't pay our licence fee, that's all I can say.

MAM: # We do. I pay it.

DAD: You what?

MAM: **Jim, they've got detector vans now.**

DAD: ## Detector vans my arse.

MAM: **Ooh, they come and park outside your house, they even know which programme you're watching.**

DAD: **Yes well, they wouldn't charge us if they knew we were watching that shite. Bloody Changing bloody Rooms. More like changing bloody channels.**

MAM: **Well I like seeing people's houses get done up. It's very popular is this, Jim.**

DAD: **Why don't they do an hour and a half's film of me emulsioning the bloody box-room**

MAM: **Huh! When was the last time you did any decorating?**

DAD: **Well I'm waiting for them Changing Rooms clowns, aren't I? Eh? Like them two there, they're doing bugger all, just sitting on their arses.**

MAM: ## I'd be ashamed to let anybody come to this house.

PAUSE. THEY WATCH – WE SEE LAWRENCE

DAD: **I wouldn't let old nancy-boy round here for a kick-off.**

MAM: # Ooh. I think I might stencil our kitchen unit.

DAD: **Stencil my arse.** POINTS **He would, there's nothing he'd like better than to stencil my arse.**

LIVING ROOM. DAVE AND DENISE HAVE ARRIVED. ANTONY IS IN THE KITCHEN LOOKING FOR BISCUITS

ANTONY: oov **Shall I open the Wagon Wheels.**

DAD/ DAVE/ MAM: # No.

DENISE: # Yeah.

ANTONY: ## Kit Kats?

DENISE/ DAD/ MAM/ DAVE: # No

DAD: # Just bring us a Penguin.

DENISE: ## Can't we open them all?

MAM: I'm only opening one packet. If I open more than one packet it'll get ate. That's the trouble in this house – every time I open something it disappears.

DENISE: ## The baby wants a Wagon Wheel.

MAM: Aah. SHOUTS TO ANTONY **Antony, open the Wagon Wheels, don't open the Kit Kats. There're some Penguins and some Club biscuits already open**

DAVE: SHOUTS TO ANTONY **Ey, and save some biscuits for next week for Nana and Homo.**

MAM: **What did I call Homo before?**

DAVE: **Homer.**

MAM: **Oh yeah, oh what am I like?** TO ANTONY **Eh just one.**
ANTONY COMES IN WITH BISCUITS

MAM: **Do you want one Dave?**

DAVE: **Oh yeah, I'll have a Club please, ta.**

MAM: TO DENISE **Wagon Wheel.** TO JIM **Penguin.**

DAD: **Thank you.**

MAM: **I'll have this one.**

DAVE: SINGS **'If you like a lot of chocolate on your biscuit join our Club'**
DENISE LAUGHS.

DAD: **If you're feeling p-p-p-peckish, p-p-p-pick up a Penguin!'**

MAM: SINGS **'Only the crumbliest, flakiest chocolate, tastes like chocolate never tasted before.'**

DAD: **Who remembers this one?** SINGS

'She flies like a bird in the sky...'

DAD/ DENISE/ DAVE/ MAM:

ALL JOIN IN

'She flies like a bird and I wish that she was mine. She flies like a bird, oh me, oh my I've seen her fly, now I know, I can't let Maggie go.'

DAD: For two points Dave, what was that advert for?

DAVE: **Nimble. 'Real bread, but lighter'**

DAD: **Correct.**

DAVE: **Whooh.**

DAD: **Correct young man.**

PAUSE. THEY ALL EAT CHOCOLATE BISCUITS.

DAD: Do you know what the best advert was, bar none: Cadbury's Smash. ROBOT'S VOICE

'We peel them with our steely knives.'

MAM: Aah, you know the one I like the best, that tea ad with all the chimps.

ALL: **Ah yeah.**

MAM: **How do they get them to do that, Jim?**

DAD: I don't know, but I tell you what, I wish I could get them chimp trainers to spend a couple of weeks with our Antony teaching him how to make a proper bloody brew.

Episode 4

 **KITCHEN. DENISE, CHERYL, MAM.
NANA HAS COME TO STAY AFTER HER CATARACT
OPERATION MUCH TO JIM'S DISGUST**

DENISE: Ey, right, did anyone see that film last night about the tattoos?

MAM: No.

DENISE: It was absolutely brilliant. There was this bloke, right, and he was obsessed with this woman what was a model and he kidnapped her and he drugged her and then he covered her whole body from the neck downwards with a tattoo.

MAM: Did she not like it?

DENISE: No.

MAM: I'd hate that to happen to me.

CHERYL: What happened at the end?

DENISE: When he'd completely finished her tattoo, right, he took his clothes off and he had a matching body tattoo – and then they were doing it, and his tattoo and her tattoo mingled into one.

CHERYL: Did they?

DENISE: But then she grabbed the tattoo gun and stabbed him with it.

MAM: Oooh.

CHERYL: **Blimey.**

DENISE: There was all ink everywhere.

MAM: Oooh, what a thing to happen.

CHERYL: I'd love another Club if you've got one, Barbara.

CUT TO LIVING ROOM

DAVE: **He tattooed the whole of her body.**

DAD: **What, boobs 'n' all?**

DAVE: Oh, the full monty.

DAD: Well, I don't see the point of that. You'd wanna be looking at them, not covering them up.

DAVE: My point exactly, James.

BARBARA COMES IN AND SITS DOWN

MAM: **Aah, she still asleep?**

DAD: Yeah. She's got jaw-ache, God love her.

MAM: Y'all right, Dave?

DAVE: Yeah.

MAM: You had your tea?

DAVE: No, I'm gonna stop for some chips on't way home. Denise couldn't be bothered cooking me owt.

MAM: **Well don't forget, she is pregnant.**

DAD: Bloody 'ell, Barbara, there's no chance of us forgetting is there?

LOOKS AT NANA

I don't know where she inherits this lazy streak from.

PAUSE

MAM: Ooh, ey, Dave, Denise has just been telling us about that film last night.

DAVE: **Did you watch it, Barbara?**

MAM: **No.**

DAVE: Brilliant it was. This bloke kidnapped this woman and drugged her, then tattooed her from the neck down.

MAM: Ooh, in't it awful – when you weigh up? Was she a young girl, Dave?

DAVE: **Oh yeah. She was a model.**

DAD: **Was she? What was it called?**

DAVE: **Tattoo.**

DAD: 'Hey, Boss, the plane.'

CUT

DAVE LAUGHS

LIVING ROOM.

NANA IS STILL ASLEEP AND GIVES A LITTLE SNORE.

DAD: Ey, Dave.

DAVE: Yeah?

DAD: Can you bring the car round on Sunday to take Norma back, I mean, er,

I don't like the idea of her on the
bus with her eye-patch.
It doesn't seem right.

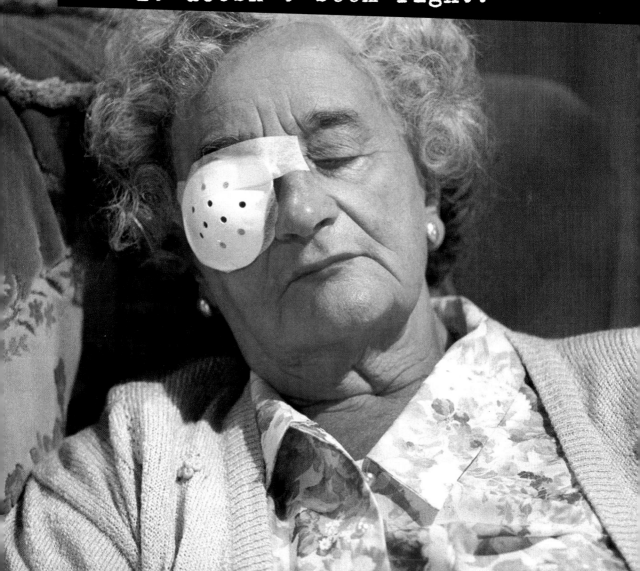

DAVE: Yeah, no bother. What time d'you want me round?

MAM: Don't worry about it, Dave – to be honest I think she'll need to stay another week.

DAD: **Another bloody week! Over my dead body.**

MAM: # Jim! She thinks the world of you.

DAD: Thinks the bloody world of me? Today, she had a family size bag of bloody Revels and did she offer me one? Did she shite. She sat there on her big fat arse announcing every one that she put in her big fat gob. 'Oh, coconut! Oh, orange! Oh, Malt-bloody-teser...'

MAM: Oh, is that it then? We can't look after my own mother because she wouldn't share a bag of Revels. Grow up, Jim.

DAD: Me grow up? She makes me un-bloody-plug everything at night before we go to bed – but she's got herself a bloody electric blanket on all night.

MAM: Oooh, Jim. If it was your mam and dad, God rest their souls, I'd've done anything for 'em.

DAD: # She should be in a bloody home.

MAM: She is in a home. She's in our home. And that's where she's staying – with a family that loves her.

JIM SULKS

DAD: MUMBLES 'Ooooh caramel, I think! No, wait, not caramel, coffee! Coffee one that was...' Greedy old cow...

Episode 5

 DAVE AND DAD ARE IN THE LIVING ROOM. DENISE AND MAM ARE IN THE KITCHEN.

BARBARA IS FEELING VERY RESENTFUL. DAD BLAMES THE MENOPAUSE

MAM: I'm just his bloody skivvy. It was worse when your nana was staying – I'd come home from work and that sink would be full of pots, they'd be fighting and I just wanted to get my coat and go somewhere.

DENISE: Aah, Mam. He's just so lazy.

MAM: Well he hasn't got any hobbies. I try and think of things for him to do. He does the crossword in the paper right, so I bought him a Puzzler the other day and he just went mad, he said I'd wasted one pund seventy and he wouldn't speak to me for the rest of the night. It's not a life this, it's just a bloody existence.

DENISE: And he's always got food stuck in his beard.

MAM: Well he never has a wash.

CUT TO JIM AND DAVE IN THE FRONT ROOM

DAD: How long does it last, this change malarky?

DAVE: Dunno. Few years in't it?

DAD: **Bloody 'ell.**

CUT TO DENISE AND BARBARA IN THE KITCHEN

MAM: The only time he has a wash is when he goes to the doctor's. He just sits there mouthing off in that chair. Another time I came in, your nana's face was like thunder – he wouldn't put her drops in.

DENISE: **He's so selfish.**

MAM: Poor Antony, got no confidence – Jim's knocked it all out of him, calling him a lanky streak of piss all the time.

DENISE: Well, well he has got a point there.

CUT TO JIM AND DAVE IN THE FRONT ROOM.

DAD: **Has your mum had her change yet?**

DAVE: **Dunno – she's not said nowt.**

CUT TO BARBARA AND DENISE IN THE KITCHEN

MAM: You know, most of the time, most of the time I put up with it – while you two were growing up.

DENISE: Ah.

MAM: **Now I don't know why I'm here Denise**

DENISE: Ah, Mam, ah. You could come and live with us. No you could.

MAM: Ah, Denise.

DENISE: 'Cause when that baby's born I'm gonna be rushed off my feet. Ey.

CUT TO JIM AND DAVE IN THE FRONT ROOM

DAD: Tell you what, Dave, you should have seen her before. She's gone too far this time.

DAVE: Why?

DAD: # Bang. She just switched the bloody telly off.

DAVE: ## No need for that.

DAD: That's what I mean.

JIM: I'm not one of them husbands that goes out every night. Admittedly I would be if I could afford it. I have two nights and one afternoon a week and it's still not bloody good enough.

DAVE: I don't wanna get involved me, Jim. She does work hard though.

DAD: ## Hard my arse. A couple of hours in a bloody bakery.

DAVE: I don't wanna get involved. It's nowt to do with me.

DAD: The trouble with me lad, is I'm too easy-bloody-going. She walks all over me. I mean the days she does work in the bakery it can be half seven, quarter to eight, before my tea's ready.

But I don't say nothing, I just get on with it.

CUT TO KITCHEN

MAM: He's got no conversation about him at all. Do you know he absolutely hated work. Hated it. I always thought that when he gave it up, I'd see a lovely side of Jim that I'd never seen before. There isn't one.

DENISE: No.

MAM: You know what the doctor said about this HRT thing. He said have a little think and go and discuss it with your husband. All Jim could say was that HRT's horse's piss and that them doctors are raking it in.

DENISE AND DAD HAVE BEEN ARGUING, DAVE UNWISELY INTERVENES

DENISE: **Dave, will you keep your big fat nose out.** It's nothing to do with you. It's not your family.

DAVE: Well, you've brought me in on this argument, haven't you. It's nothing to do with me. Bloody 'ell. Anyway, what about you having a pop at your Dad and you're never off your arse, are you?

DAD: **Cor-rect David.**

DENISE: I'm pregnant and I'm carrying your child about, thank you very much.

DAVE: What d'you mean you're pregnant, you're carrying my child about thank you very much? Anyone'd think you were the only woman ever to bloody be pregnant. It's only the size of a bloody orange.

DENISE: Well that's as much as you know – it's the size of a grapefruit, thank you, Dave.

DAD: **Grapefruit my arse.**

DAVE: **Cor-rect Jim.** TO DENISE

DAD: Thank you.

DAVE: Anyway, how come we never go round to my mum and dad's?

DENISE: Well, I'll tell you why, Dave – 'cause they sit on their arses and watch telly all night and it's boring. Anyway, you go round twice a week as it is

DAVE: That's to take me washing round and go back and pick it up again – you know that.

DENISE: Oh well, well, well how come we've been married ages and your mum's never offered to do my washing.

DAVE: Well you've got a washing machine, you should be doing my washing. Cost me two hundred and eighty notes that.

DAD: # How much?

DAVE: Two hundred and eighty five bloody notes and she's never had a single thing in it.

DENISE: ## Well you try being pregnant right and...

DAVE: And what? And nothing. You're bone bloody idle.

DENISE: ## I am preparing myself for motherhood.

DAVE: Mother my arse.

DAD: ## Cor-rect, Dave.

DAVE: Thank you James.

DAD: Who's 'em... Who's gonna wash the baby's things, Dave?

DENISE: Will you stop shit-stirring it, Dad. It's nothing to do with you.

THEY HEAR THE FRONT DOOR SLAM. DENISE GOES TO THE WINDOW AND LOOKS OUT.

DENISE: It's me mam. She's got her coat on. Dad, will you go after her?

DAD: Me, go after her, why don't you go after her?

DENISE: ## I'm pregnant! Dave, you go after her.

DAVE: I'm watching this.

JIM: She's probably gone to Mary's – to have a bloody go at me from round there. Anyway, Mary's the only one who doesn't know I'm a big, fat, lazy arse.

SILENCE. DENISE IS STILL AT THE WINDOW.

DENISE: She's not gone to Mary's. I wonder where she's going? It's all your fault. She's on the change – she might walk out in front of a lorry and get run over.

DAD: Well, we could always put a claim in.

DENISE: Poor mam, I've never seen her so upset. You're horrible, you. You've broke our home up.

DAD: It's not even your bloody home, you don't live here.

DENISE: Mam said Antony stormed out. Now she's gone. I'll be next.

DAD: You're too bloody lazy to storm off anywhere, you.

DENISE: No you're the lazy one.

DAD: ## You're the bloody lazy one.

DENISE: ## Get lost – you're way lazier than me.

           PAUSE

DAD: ## My arse. You are.

DENISE: No you are.

DAD: TO DAVE ## She is.

DENISE: TO DAVE ## He is.

           JIM TURNS OVER. WHO WANTS TO BE A MILLIONAIRE? IS ON. HE RUBS HIS HANDS IN GLEE

ALL: # Waaay.

DAD: I tell you what, this is got to be the best bloody show on the television, bar none.

DAVE: RUBS HANDS TOGETHER **Too right.**

CUT

JIM, DENISE, DAVE ARE STILL WATCHING WHO WANTS TO BE A MILLIONAIRE. BARBARA RETURNS.

MAM: Ta DENISE HANDS HER A CIGGY Ta.

DENISE: You all right, Mam?

MAM: Yeah.

DAVE: You all right, Barbara?

MAM: Yeah.

DAD: You're all right, Barb?

MAM: I have to be don't I?

DAD: I've walked the length of this neighbourhood looking for you. You've had us worried out of our bloody minds 'ere.

DENISE: Where did you go, Mam?

MAM: I just went for a little walk – to clear my head.

DENISE: Anything the matter, Mam?

MAM: No nothing. Nothing that won't keep. I've kept it in for over twenty-seven years now.

DAD: I'll tell you what, Barb, there was a woman just like you, on the change. She made a thousand pounds there on the telly So it's not all doom and gloom. Look, you and your change, you just sit there and I'll make us a nice cup of tea.

THEY ALL LOOK AT JIM IN DISBELIEF.

DAD: A nice cup of tea, Barb? SHE IGNORES HIM Nice cup of tea, Dave? Denise? Nice cup of tea for you and the little one? Medium to strong, eh? I'll go and heat the pot and we'll let it brew, eh? There's a nice cup of tea coming your way. A nice cup of tea coming your way. Oh and keep an eye on Dave from Halifax for me because I am making a brew. Even though it's my favourite programme, I am making a brew. And do you know why? Because *I* am a family man.

CUT

Episode 6

LIVING ROOM. TWIGGY AND DAD.

BARBARA HAS LAID ON A BUFFET FOR ANTONY'S 18TH BIRTHDAY

TWIGGY AND DAD ARE WATCHING EASTENDERS AND BLOWING UP BALLOONS. BARBARA IS IN THE KITCHEN.

TWIGGY: HOLDS A ROUND BALLOON AT HIS BREAST

Ey, Jim, what does that remind you of?

THEY BOTH LAUGH CHILDISHLY

DAD: **Beverley Macca.**

TWIGGY: **Correct.**

JIM PLACES A LONG BALLOON AT HIS CROTCH

DAD: **Twiggy, what about this one. Oh nurse, what time's my operation?**

THEY CONTINUE BLOWING UP BALLOONS. JIM PASSES A BALLOON TO TWIGGY TO TIE UP.

DAD: **Here you are, Twigg. Do that. I tell you what, it takes it out of you this, doesn't it?**

TWIGGY: HANGS A LONG ONE WITH TWO ROUND ONES EITHER SIDE **Ey, Jim.**

DAD: OF RUDE BALLOONS **Leave that like that. It'll bloody annoy Norma.**

 EMMA AND DARREN HAVE ARRIVED.

MAM: **Oooh, Emma, would you like a drink?**

EMMA: Erm, well, I'm driving – so just an orange please.

MAM: **Oh, I don't think we've got any orange.**

Would you like a Vimto?

EMMA: Er, I'm all right thanks.

MAM: Help yourself to the buffet. Can I get you a ham sandwich.

EMMA: **Oh, no thank you, I'm a vegetarian.**

MAM: Ooh, **can I do you a Dairylea instead?**

EMMA: No, honestly, I'm fine thank you.

MAM: She can have Dairylea can't she, Denise?

DENISE: Yeah.

NANA: # What is she?

DENISE: # She's a vegetarian, Nana.

NANA: Ooh, you could have a bit of cheese though. Have you got some cheese, Barbara? Oh Emma, it's a shame for you.

DAD: Look, if she doesn't want anything, she doesn't want any. Leave the girl alone.

ANTONY: She's all right.

DAD: That's a belting little car that, love. What does your Dad drive?

NANA: Could you have some wafer-thin ham? Could she have wafer-thin ham, Barbara

MAM: No.

NANA: Ooh, do you know, we've heard nothing from Antony but Emma, Emma, Emma. It's the first time I've known Antony courting.

DENISE: Nana, don't be saying that.

NANA: Is your nana still alive, Emma?

EMMA: Yeah.

NANA: Does she live with you?

EMMA: No.

DENISE: I can smell something in here.

MAM: I've told him to put his shoes on.

DAD: It's not me.

DENISE: Can you smell it?

MAM: **Ooh! It smells like dog muck.**

NANA: **'Muck for luck'**

MAM: Who's brought that in? Is that you, Darren?

DARREN: Don't know.

MAM: **Well have a look. Somebody's walked it in.**

EVERYONE LOOKS AT THEIR SHOES

MAM: Is there anything there, Jim?

DAD: No.

DAVE: **Oh no – I think it's me. Sorry, Emma.**

EMMA: You're all right.

DENISE: Dave! Take it off, you big clown. Oh, **I'm so sorry Emma.**

DAVE: I'll leave it on to dry, then it'll be easier to get off.

DENISE: Oh, Mam, will you get his shoe off him.

NANA: **'Muck for luck'.**

ANTONY: **Sorry, Emma.**

DAVE: **Sorry, Emma.**

MAM: What a thing to happen. I am sorry, Emma.

EMMA: It's all right.

MAM: **I bet this never happens at your house, does it?**

NANA: TO DARREN **Is your nana still alive, Gary?**
DARREN: **Yeah.**

NANA: **Does she live with you, Darren?**

DARREN: **No.**

DAD: **Oh well, I'll have to nip upstairs.**

I've got a turtle's head in me underpants.

Episode 7

LIVING ROOM. THE WHOLE FAMILY.

IT'S CHRISTMAS. JIM, SPORTING PAPER HAT, CHRISTMAS CARDIGAN AND A LOOK OF DISDAIN IS WATCHING NOEL'S CHRISTMAS PRESENTS WITH DAVE AND ANTONY. NANA IS ASLEEP WEARING HER PAPER HAT. BARBARA (COMPLETE WITH PAPER HAT) HAS BEEN IN THE KITCHEN ELBOW-DEEP IN WASHING-UP. A BIG TURKEY CARCASS SITS IN THE MIDDLE OF THE KITCHEN TABLE. DENISE IS VERY PREGNANT AND HAS JUST COME DOWNSTAIRS AFTER A NAP

MAM: **Oh, ey Antony, what time are you going to Emma's?**

ANTONY: Well her mam said five for five-thirty,
so I think that means about quarter-past.

MAM: Ooh, ooh Antony, in't it funny you having to have two Christmas dinners.

ANTONY: **Yeah s'all right really – well they're vegetarians,**

so they're having nut roast.

DAD: The tight gets. All that money and they won't fork out for a bit of turkey.

NANA: I can't believe they're having their Christmas dinner at night. Lay heavy on 'em, won't it.

MAM: Yeah. Will you be staying late, Antony?

ANTONY: Yeah. Well, after they've had their dinner they always play charades, y'know, and parlour games 'n' that.

THEY ALL KILL THEMSELVES LAUGHING

DAD: Parlour games!

DENISE: Is their telly broke?

EVERYONE LAUGHS

DAD: Parlour games my arse. Ey, tell you what you'd be good at, that's if they play it – hunt the Giro.

MAM: Well I think they're right. We could do that – play some sort of game. Ey Denise, do you remember that Christmas when we tried to play Rummy and your nana had two kings in her handbag.

NANA: I didn't know they were there, Barbara – but they did come in handy for that Royal Flush and I won 13 pounds off Jim that night.

MAM: Oh yes. Ey Jim, wasn't that the Christmas you didn't sleep.

DAD: Anyway, what do you want to go round there for, for all that bloody shite, when you could be here with us watching the bloody box? Parlour games my arse – they want to get out a bit more that lot.

MAM: Let's all have a snowball? Don't snowballs make you feel Christmassy, ey?

DAD: **Snowballs my arse.** It's a bloody swizz this Christmas lark.

MAM: Denise?

DENISE: Yeah.

MAM: Have you decided yet what you're going to do for the Millennium?

DENISE: Well, we talked about it for ages, didn't we Dave?

DAVE: Umm.

DENISE: In the end we decided we'd just come round here, really.

MAM: Ah.

DAVE: Um. Round here.

MAM: Ah.

DENISE: **You still doing a buffet?**

MAM: Oh yeah. We've invited Mary and Joe and Cheryl.

DAD: Bloody 'ell. I hope you haven't invited Cheryl's bloody mate. There'll be no buffet left for us, if she gets at it. The big lazy heifer.

MAM: Mary's really looking forward to it, Joe's not really bothered. She said he can't get excited about the Millennium.

DAD: Bloody 'ell, that's a surprise, isn't it. Millennium my arse. It's just another bloody swizz they've come up with to bloody rip me off, isn't it. Well I'm gonna treat it like any other New Year's Eve, me. That's it. I'm gonna get totally bladdered and I'm doing nothing else, that's it, I'm doing nothing else. They can take it or leave it.

DAD: Tony bloody Blair – and his show who've bloody organised it. It's all a bloody con to get more money out of me.

DENISE: **Who can, Dad?**

CUT

DAVE HAS TAKEN NANA BACK TO HER HOUSE. DENISE IS UPSTAIRS IN THE BATHROOM.

DENISE: OOV **Mam! Will you come up!**

IN THE LIVING ROOM JIM TRUPS AND WAFTS IT AWAY, DISGUSTED BY THE SMELL. BARBARA GOES TO THE BATHROOM WHERE DENISE IS CRYING. WE ONLY SEE HER HEAD AND SHOULDERS, BUT SHE'S OBVIOUSLY SITTING ON THE TOILET.

DENISE: **Oh Mam, a load of water's came out. I think my waters have broken – and Dave's not even here.**

MAM: **Oh Denise! Oh my God, Denise! Oh Denise. Oh love. Wait there – I'll go and ring Dave on the mobile.**

DENISE: **Yeah. Yeah. Yeah. I've got the mobile.**

MAM: **Oh God, Denise.**
Well I'll go an ring the hospital and I'll send your dad up. Jim!

DENISE: **Yeah, yeah.**

MAM: **Jim!**

DENISE: **Mam, don't leave me.**

BARBARA RUNS DOWNSTAIRS INTO THE LIVING ROOM.

MAM: **Jim, get upstairs, our Denise's waters have broken.**

DAD: # What's broken, Barb?

MAM: **Her waters. Get upstairs and calm her down. She's all upset 'cause Dave's not here. Here, take her this, this birthing tape, go on, the tape's already in there. Come on now.** BARBARA HANDS JIM TAPE MACHINE AND TAPE

DAD: **Bloody 'ell Barb, what is it, the bloody Dambusters and Dave would have been here only for your bloody mother.**

AS JIM GOES UP THE STAIRS HE HUMS THE THEME TO THE DAMBUSTERS

DAD: **Denise it's your dad, love.**

DENISE: Come in, Dad. Come in.

DAD: # It's not too messy is it?

DENISE: No. Come in.

HE GOES IN. DENISE IS SITTING ON THE EDGE OF THE BATH, DOUBLED OVER. JIM PUTS THE TOILET SEAT DOWN AND SITS ON IT, COMFORTING HIS SOBBING DAUGHTER

DAD: You're all right. What's the matter?

DENISE: I don't know, I can't even remember what I'm supposed to be doing out of me baby book. I'm supposed to be doing me breathing, but I can't even remember how to breathe.

DAD: Come on, you'll be all right. Here y'are, let's play your tape, eh?

CHARLOTTE CHURCH'S PIE JESU PLAYS IN THE BACKGROUND

DENISE: Yeah.

DAD: **Are you definitely sure it wasn't just a great big piss, love.**

DENISE: **No, I know it wasn't.**

SILENCE AS PIE JESU PLAYS.

DENISE: I don't know what I'm gonna do and Dave's gonna miss it and he's supposed to be helping me with me breathing and counting 'em, them... things what I'm having. REALLY SOBBING Dad, I'm so scared and I don't even think I want the baby any more. And I don't think Dave wants it either – he didn't even want to feel it kicking before and I be ya he'll leave it all to me and I don't even know anything about babies.

DAD: **You'll be all right. There's nothing to it.**

DENISE: What if the baby doesn't like me? What if I don't like the baby?

DAD: Of course you'll like it – you'll love it. I remember the first time when your mam put you in my arms and I looked at you, oh God you were beautiful and I knew, I knew then, I'd do anything for you, anything for you and our Antony.

DENISE: What if I'm not a good mam like me mam?

DAD: **You'll be a wonderful mother.**

DENISE: Dad, if Dave don't come back, will you come with me to the hospital?

DAD: Of course I will, I'll be right there outside. But your mam will be inside with you.

DENISE: **You promise you will, Dad? You will stay with me?**

DAD: Of course I'll stay with you, I'll always be there for you. Ey Denise, I'm gonna be a granddad.

BARBARA COMES IN

MAM: **I've rang the hospital and they've told me to tell you to come in, so I've rang a taxi and it's on its way.**

DAD: **Bloody 'ell Barb,**

it's double fare on Christmas Day. CUT

I give you David

SERIES THREE

The Royle
Heir

SERIES THREE – THE CAST

Denise Royle		Caroline Aherne
Dave Best		Craig Cash
PJ		John Delaney
Twiggy		Geoffrey Hughes
Baby David		James & Matthew Hughes
Barbara Royle	(Mam)	Sue Johnston
Mary Carroll		Doreen Keogh
Michelle		Sally Lindsay
Antony Royle		Ralph Little
Joe Carroll		Peter Martin
Norma Speakman	(Nana)	Liz Smith
Emma		Sheridan Smith
Cheryl Carroll		Jessica Stevenson
Jim Royle	(Dad)	Ricky Tomlinson
Darren		Andrew Whyment

Episode 1

 LIVING ROOM. MAM AND DAD. MAM HAS JUST CUT DAD'S HAIR

DAD: You get better looking every day. I'll never get tired of looking at you. Oh you're gorgeous you are. KISSES HIMSELF AGAIN

Ta Barb. Saved a nice couple of quid there love.

MAM: I'll sweep up when I've got a minute.

THEN SHE SITS DOWN TO WATCH THE TELEVISION. WATCHDOG IS ON

MAM: Oh Jim is there owt on?

DAD: Nah the usual shite. We're gonna have to get Sky you know Barb.

MAM: Oh Jim, we don't want Sky. We don't watch telly enough to get the value.

CUT

DENISE AND DAVE ARRIVE. DENISE IS CARRYING A SMALL HANDBAG. DAVE IS LOADED DOWN WITH BABY THINGS IN MATERNITY BAGS AND CARRIES A PORTABLE CAR SEAT/ROCKER WITH BABY DAVID IN

DENISE: Hiya Dad.

DAD: Bloody hell it's Posh and Becks.

MAM: How's the sleeping going, Denise?

DENISE: Well I slept all through last night.

MAM: No, I mean Baby David.

DENISE: Oh. Dunno.

DAVE: He woke up twice last night Barbara.

 ANTONY AND DARREN ENTER. DENISE IS BREASTFEEDING

MAM: Ooh hiya Darren, you alright? Oh Darren we haven't seen you for a long time. Are you still working?

DARREN: No.

MAM: Ooh what happened there then? That was a good job in that warehouse.

DARREN: Eh, they fired me off.

MAM: Why?

DARREN: They caught me nickin'

DAD: You daft sod. What was you nicking?

DARREN: **A fridge freezer.**

DAD: Well, they're not easy to get up your bloody jumper, are they?

 CONVERSATION CONTINUES...

DAD: **When's your Kenny due out of the nick Darren?**

DARREN: I dunno.

DAD: Must be soon though mustn't it lad?

DARREN: Don't know.

DAD: **Is he coming back round 'ere to live?**

DARREN: **No he can't.**

DAD: Yeah, best not to, ey.

MAM: Ey Darren, you want to watch yourself, nicking fridges, you'll end up inside with all your other brothers.

DARREN: It was a fridge freezer Barbara.

MAM: Ooh.

ANTONY: Come and get some scran Darren.

AS HE PASSES, DARREN CAN'T KEEP HIS EYES OFF DENISE'S BREAST. ANTONY IS HALVING SAUSAGES AND MASH AND BUTTERING BREAD

DARREN: **Hey did you see your kid then?**

ANTONY: What?

DARREN: She had her tit out.

ANTONY: **Well yeah, she was feeding the baby.**

DARREN: Does she do that a lot?

ANTONY: Yeah.

DARREN: **She always use the same tit?**

LIVING ROOM

BABY DAVID DOES A BABY DAVID FART

DAD: `That's my boy! Oh he's a Royle all right!`

DAVE PICKS UP BABY DAVID

DAVE: Well I hope it's not followed through. Oh let me just smell your bum bum. Oh I think he might have done one Denise, have a smell.

DAVE PASSES BABY DAVID TO DENISE WHO PASSES HIM ON TO BARBARA.

DENISE: Here y'are. I'm not sure. Mam?

BARBARA SMELLS THE ARSE OF BABY DAVID.

MAM: Oh. Oh yeah. Definitely has.

BARBARA PASSES BABY DAVID BACK TO DENISE.

DENISE: Yeah he has.

SHE PASSES HIM BACK TO DAVE.

DAVE: Oh, he's definitely done one.

DENISE: He's gonna need changing in't he. SHOUTING INTO KITCHEN Antony!

 LIVING ROOM.

DENISE: Oh yeah, hey Mam guess what.

MAM: What?

DENISE: You know Dave.

MAM: Yeah.

DENISE: Um, he's making a little farmyard for Baby David.

MAM: Is he?

DENISE: Yeah.

MAM: Are you Dave?

DAVE: **Yeah.**

MAM: Oh how lovely, what you making it out of?

DAVE: **A bit of scrap wood I've got.**

MAM: Oh. What have you done so far?

DAVE: Well, I've made a little gate, you know, to keep the animals in.

MAM: Have you got any animals?

DAVE: No, I've not made them yet.

DAD: Well what the bloody 'ell are you making the gate for lad?
Come on son, get a grip of yourself.

MAM: Oh Dave, when you get to the sheep, give me a shout 'cause I've got an old ball of Arran wool in the airing cupboard doing nothing.

DAVE: I wasn't really thinking of having sheep, Barbara.

MAM: Oh why, what you thinking of having?

DAVE: **Well, you know, ducks and livestock.**

DAD: If you're having a pig Dave, we could always get Cheryl to model for it.

DENISE: Dad.

PAUSE

MAM: **Are you having chickens, Dave?**

DAVE: Where?

MAM: **In your farmyard.**

DAVE: Oh more than likely Barbara.

MAM: **Aah. Aah.** SINGS UNDER HER BREATH **Chick, chick, chicken.**

Episode 2

 LIVING ROOM. ANTONY, MAM, BABY DAVID. MAM HAS BEEN LOOKING AFTER BABY DAVID FOR THE NIGHT.

DAVE AND DENISE ENTER AND SIT DOWN. ALL WATCH TV – LONG PAUSE

MAM: **Oh ey, you two look a bit rough.**

DENISE: **Oh yeah.** TO BABY DAVID **Hiya!**

MAM: **Oh, didn't have a peep out of him all night.**

DENISE: **Out of who?**

MAM: **Baby David.**

DENISE: **Aah.**

MAM: **Aah, who'd like a bacon butty?**

DENISE/
DAVE: **Oh, yes please.**

MAM: **Antony, go and put some bacon under love.**

ANTONY GOES

DENISE: Dave?

DAVE: Umm?

DENISE: Will you take Baby David upstairs or somewhere so I can have a ciggy?

DAVE: **I'm watching Ant 'n' Dec.**

DENISE: Dave!

DAVE: **Come on then sunshine.**

DAVE LEAVES SINGING 'YOU ARE MY SUNSHINE'

MAM: Do you know Denise, you're really good about that not smoking in front of Baby David.

DENISE: Yeah I know, but I'm only doing it until he's old enough to be able to walk out the room himself and then, then it's up to him, in it?

MAM: **Yeah. Oh you are a good mother Denise.**

DENISE: Aah. Ta.

CUT

ACTION

LIVING ROOM. BABY DAVID IS ASLEEP UPSTAIRS. JIM HAS COME DOWNSTAIRS

DAD: Oh ey Dave, you know that little farmyard you're making for Baby David.

DAVE: Umm.

DENISE: Yeah.

DAD: **How's that coming along?**

DAVE: Oh alright thanks yeah.

DENISE: **He's made a pond for it. It's absolutely brilliant.**

MAM: Oh have you Dave?

DAVE: Umm.

MAM: **What for the ducks?**

DAVE: Yeah.

DAD: Ah yeah. What did you make that out of Dave?

DAVE: Well. I just put some glue on the back of one of Denise's old vanity mirrors. You know. But I stuck the wrong side down so the ducks are a bit too magnified.

MAM: Aah.

JIM GIVES DAVE A LOOK

DAVE: And I bought a frog as well but that's turned out to be bigger than th ducks.

DAD: **Bloody hell, Dave.**

DENISE: I told you to take the ducks with you when you were buying the frog

DAVE: But they're stuck down Denise. I can't go carting the whole farmyard around with me can I?

DAD: Bloody Hell!

DENISE: **Well you never made us one when we were little.**

DAD: Well that's just as well isn't it, with bloody killer frogs on the loose.

CUT

ANTONY HAS BROUGHT IN THE BACON BUTTIES. THEY ARE ALL EATING.

ANTONY: ANTONY LOOKS OUT OF THE WINDOW
Hey. Mary and Joe are getting out of a taxi.

DAVE: # A taxi!

ANTONY: **Yeah.**

BARBARA STANDS UP AND GOES TO WINDOW

DENISE: **A taxi!**

ANTONY: **Yeah.**

DAD: # A bloody taxi!

ANTONY: **Yeah.**

MAM: **Where've they been?**

BARBARA GOES TO THE FRONT DOOR

MAM: SHOUTING TO MARY **Mary, Mary, what's to do?**

MARY: OOV **Oh Barbara.**

MAM: **Ohhh Mary, oh come on, come on in. Go in Joe.** TO EVERYONE IN ROOM **Ey, Joe's all bandaged up. Come in Joe, come in Mary, go on Joe, come on. Antony will you get out of that chair. Go on Joe.**

EVERYBODY SHOOTS LOOKS AT EVERYONE ELSE AS MARY AND JOE ARRIVE IN COATS. JOE HAS HIS TWO FINGERS ON HIS RIGHT HAND BANDAGED.

MARY: **Oh Barbara.**

MAM: **Sit down Joe.**

MARY: **It's been a terrible morning. We've been down to casualty with Joe.**

MAM: ## Oh. What's to do Joe?

MARY: ### It's his two fingers on his right hand.
Three-and-a-half hours in casualty, Barbara.

MAM: **Oh, how did you do it, Joe?**

MARY: He was grating a bit of cheese, Barbara. It could happen to anyone.

JIM GIVES DAVE A LOOK

JOE: They were letting people who came in after me go before me.

MARY: Yes, but they had heart attacks Joe.
Do you know Barbara, they kept us waiting so long that in the end it was only my Joe left and a little boy who had a marble lodged up his nose.

MAM: Antony, Antony go and get Joe a Kit Kat. Did he have a tetanus, Mary?

ANTONY GOES TO KITCHEN

MARY: Oh yes Barbara. Just a little prick in his bottom.

DAVE CATCHES JIM'S EYE

MARY: Barbara, isn't the NHS terrible, I mean just terrible? They had no interest in Joe at all.

DAD: I hope that's not the old er arse wiping hand is it, Joe?

MAM: Jim!

ANTONY COMES BACK WITH KIT KAT AND GIVES IT TO JOE

JOE: Oh aye. Oh Cheers.

MAM: Oh, I don't know. All this palaver over grating some cheese.

MARY: Oh I think we'll be going back to Dairylea Barbara. It's a much safer cheese.

MAM: Oh yeah.

MARY: We've just got to hope and pray now that the skin grows back over the tops.

MAM: What did they say at the hospital, Mary?

MARY: They told me to keep him warm and dry. It seems so unfair Barbara. The cheese wasn't even for him. It was for Cheryl.

WE HEAR BABY DAVID CRYING OVER THE BABY MONITOR ON THE SHELF NEXT TO JIM. THEY ALL ARGUE ABOUT WHO SHOULD GO UP TO HIM.

DENISE: Oh blimey. Dave.

DAVE: Umm.

DENISE: Will you go up?

DAVE: No, I put him up.

DENISE: Mam.

MAM: Yeah.

DENISE: Would you like to go up and have a little look at your little grandson?

MAM: Ooh leave him for a bit. He'll be alright.

DENISE: Yeah.

PAUSE. WATCH TV. BABY DAVID CARRIES ON CRYING

DENISE: Ohhh. I can't bear hearing him like that. D'you want a ciggy?

MAM: Oh yes please.

DENISE: **Antony. Will you go up?**

ANTONY: **Kiss my arse.**

DAD: 'Ey Baldy! That's my grandson you're talking about. Now get up there and see to him. You lazy little sod.

ANTONY LEAVES IN A HUFF.

DAD: **God, he's one lazy little get him.**

DENISE: I can't believe our Antony, he'd have left him crying all day. And he's his uncle.

DAD: Dave, d'you fancy a little eh Saturday lunchtime drinkie-poos with you old Father-in-law?

DAVE: Oh good idea that, Jim, yeah, hair of the dog.

DENISE: Oh, I fancy that, couple of pints would really sort me head out. D'you want to come Mam?

MAM: Oh I can't, can I? What about Baby David?

DAVE: Oh yeah. What about Baby David?

DENISE: Well we can leave him with Antony. You just said he's really good with him.

BARBARA, JIM, DENISE AND DAVID SNEAK OUT OF THE FRONT DOOR AND CLOSE IT BEHIND THEM. ANTONY (HOLDING BABY DAVID) COMES DOWN THE STAIRS AND INTO THE EMPTY FRONT ROOM

ANTONY:

Oh shit!

CU:

Episode 3

LIVING ROOM. DAD AND TWIGGY.

SATURDAY AFTERNOON. THE TV IS OFF AND THE RADIO IS TUNED TO A MUSIC STATION. JIM AND TWIGGY ARE STRIPPING WALLPAPER BY THE HI-FI/DRINKS CABINET. JIM IS IN HIS VEST. THEY ARE BOTH SAT DOWN HAVING A BREATHER

TWIGGY: **Would Dave not have given you a hand with this, Jim?**

DAD: **No, he's under Denise's bloody thumb in't he, the lanky streak of piss. Seen him carrying the baby around all the bloody time. I never ever picked me kids up. Unless they fell over.**

TWIGGY: **Me neither.**

DAD: **No, he's a bloody old woman with that baby. Twice last week he had the emergency doctor out to Baby David. Oh Denise was bloody fuming – he woke her up both times didn't he. No, he's completely under her bloody thumb lad.**

TWIGGY: **Always has been, Jim.**

DAD: # She says shit, he jumps on the shovel.

TWIGGY: **Yeah.**

DAD: **Not even any fun going for a pint with the bugger now, is it? After three pints, he's got the bloody photographs of the nipper out and he's crying his bloody eyes out. Oh and that bloody farmyard he's making for Baby David. It's doing my head in.**

TWIGGY: I'm sick of the farmyard too, Jim.

DAD: He's bloody terrified, he's always looking at his watch. He's always on edge. He's under the bloody thumb alright. He's not a bloody man.

THEY HEAR A KEY IN THE DOOR. JIM SPITS OUT HIS TEA AND HE AND TWIGGY RUSH BACK TO STRIPPING THE WALLS AS BARBARA ENTERS

JIM: Quick!

TWIGGY: # 'Ey I saw Cheryl the other night.

DAD: Where?

TWIGGY: Outside the chippy. Waiting for it to open.

JIM AND TWIGGY BURST INTO LAUGHTER. BARBARA STANDS IN THE KITCHEN DOORWAY

MAM: It is common that wallpaper. I'll be glad to get that wood chip up.

TWIGGY: Did all right there Barb. Pound a roll.

MAM: Yeah.

MAMBO NO. 5 BY LOU BEGA ('A LITTLE BIT OF MONICA...' ETC) COMES ON THE RADIO. JIM AND TWIGGY SCRAPE WALLPAPER IN TIME TO THE MUSIC AND BARBARA STARTS DANCING TO THE MUSIC AS SHE UNPACKS THE SHOPPING IN THE KITCHEN

DAD: I tell you what, he's got it sussed there with all the women old Mambo.

TWIGGY: Too right, Jim.

DAD: ## Would you like a little bit of Cheryl, Twiggy?

TWIGGY: You couldn't get a little bit of Cheryl, Jim.

THEY LAUGH

DAD: ## Have you seen the size of her belly?

TWIGGY: Ah it's not right is it, that much weight on a young girl.

PAUSE

TWIGGY: Oh ey, ey that was funny last week with Dave and the van getting the police out.

DAD: Eh? What was that? Dave, our Dave?

TWIGGY: Well didn't he say nothing about it?

DAD: No.

TWIGGY: Oh ey, I can't tell ya.

DAD: No come on Twiggy, tell us, come on.

TWIGGY: Oh no, I can't Jim, I mean he'll go mad if I tell you.

DAD: Come on Twig, I won't say nothing honest.

TWIGGY: Well all right, I'll tell you, but listen don't let him know you heard it from me all right?

DAD: Yeah, I won't say a word Twig, come on.

TWIGGY: Right, well last week Dave nipped down to the chemist round the corner in the van and then walked back home. Forgot he'd bloody drove there. So, the next morning he gets up, looks out, sees the van's missing and phones the police saying it's been robbed. Ten minutes later the police find the van outside the chemist where he'd left it the pillock. They nearly did him for wasting police time.

LIVING ROOM. ANTONY AND DARREN HAVE ARRIVED AND ARE IN THE KITCHEN. DAVE IS NOW IN FRONT ROOM WITH TWIGGY AND JIM

DAVE: Hey you know Darren in there, y'know who he's seeing don't you?

DAD: Who?

DAVE: Big Julie from Argos. The one who looks like Tina Turner. Her.

DAD: Big Julie from Argos! How old is she?

DAVE: Well late thirties or summit, 'bout 36, 37, 38, 39, summit like that.

DAD: Bloody 'ell, she's twice his age and our Darren hasn't started bloody shavin' yet.

TWIGGY: Well there's nothing wrong with that Jim, she's a divorced woman. I wouldn't mind having a pop at it meself.

DAD: Oh bugger off will ya Twiggy lad, Big Julie from Argos. Hey that big bride with our little Darren. She could have him for bloody breakfast, her. His spuds have only just dropped and that Tina Turner's already got hold of them. Are you havin' that, Dave?

STILL ON THE SUBJECT OF GIRLFRIENDS...

TWIGGY: I'll tell you what Dave, your ex was in the Feathers n' all last night.

DAVE: Who?

TWIGGY: Beverley Macca. She was looking a treat. High heels, fishnets, short white leather skirt, low cut top. Baps out. The lot. She looked the biz.

DAD: Bloody 'ell. What's her face like, Twig? I've never managed to look that high up.

JIM AND TWIGGY LAUGH. DAVE DOESN'T

DAD: I tell you what Dave, you slipped up there didn't ya, dumping her for our Denise. I wouldn't mind looking for Luxembourg there, ey Twiggy?

DAVE: What d'you mean, Jim?

DAD: Well, DOES ACTION WITH BOTH HANDS Tuning with the old chapel hat pegs. You know what I'm talking about Twiglet.

TWIGGY: I do, Jim. Hey I know you're not supposed to say this in this day and age with the Millennium and all that, but you cannot beat a great pair of knockers.

DAD: Oh, that's true lad.

TWIGGY: I mean a personality doesn't keep you warm at night does it?

DAVE: No.

TWIGGY: **I mean you can't play with a personality?**

DAD: **No.**

TWIGGY: **But you can play with a bloody big pair of baps though.**

DAD: **Too true, Twig.**

DAVE: **Yep.**

ANTONY AND DARREN COME IN

DAD: TELLING THE END OF A JOKE ...he said I take half a viagra to stop pissing on me shoes.

ANTONY: # Hiya Twig.

TWIGGY: **Alright Ant, alright Darren.**

DARREN: **Alright Twig.**

DAD: **Heloo lurchio, hello Casanova.**

JIM LEADS, BUT THEY ALL START SINGING TO DARREN

DAD/DAVE/
TWIGGY: **Your simply the best. Better than all the rest. Better than anyone. Anyone I've ever met.**

THEY THEN LAUNCH INTO PRIVATE DANCER. LED BY DAVE

DAVE/DAD/
TWIGGY: **I'm your Private Dancer, Dancer for Money, I'll do what you want me to do. I'm your Private Dancer.
Dancer for money and any old music will do.**

DAD: **Have you seen her Nutbush city limits?**

DARREN BURSTS INTO LAUGHTER

Episode 4

 LIVING ROOM. EARLY EVENING. THE TV IS OFF. WE HEAR NANA SOBBING AND BARBARA GENTLY COMFORTING HER.

NANA: Oh Barbara, you know, I'd always thought I'd be the first to go you kno

MAM: Oh Mam, come on now. Come on. Shh, it'll be all right. Shh.

PAUSE. CRYING. JIM WALKS IN AND SITS IN HIS CHAIR. HE LOOKS AT THE SOFA AND PUTS THE TV ON STRAIGHT AWAY

NANA: Weren't they lovely Barbara, them voluvent. What was in 'em? It was a sort of a mushroomy thing, weren't it?

MAM: **Mushrooms Mam.**

NANA: Was it?

MAM: Yeah.

NANA: **I thought it was. Hey, can I have them when I go, Barbara?**

JIM CROSSES HIS FINGERS AND LOOKS HEAVENWARDS

MAM: **Oh, I thought you wanted melon boats like we had at Denise's wedding?**

NANA: **Well yes I do, I do, but can I have them as well do you think?**

MAM: **Yeah, course you can.**

NANA: **Ohhh d'you know I, I just feel like I'm all on me own now without Elsie next door, God rest her soul. I used to let meself in to her place with a key you know and p'haps just wipe her mouth with a cloth or summit. Well it was contact wasn't it?**

MAM: **Yeah**

NANA'S THOUGHTS HAVE TURNED TO ELSIE'S BELONGINGS

DENISE AND CHERYL HAVE RETURNED FROM THE PRECINCT

NANA: **I wonder what will happen to Elsie's telly now. Her telly was two inches bigger than mine, you know.**

MAM: **Oooh.**

NANA: **And the reds were redder.**

JIM: **Bloody hell. She hasn't got more bottles of Guinness perishing away has she.**

DENISE: **Nana did Elsie have a copy of the Radio Times? A recent one?**

NANA: **I don't' know love. I'll er, I'll have a look but er, I don't like to root you know.**

MAM: **Mam I really like that set of pans that Elsie had.**

NANA: **Ohhh I know. Non stick.**

MAM: Oh were they?

NANA: Aye. Shall I bring them back here?

MAM: Oh yeah

NANA: Oh Yeah. Marion will be awash with pans so it will help her when she's sorting out TO CHERYL. She's very high up in North West Water you know.

DAD: **Did Elsie say you could have all them things Norma?**

NANA: Well she got very confused in the end, but I don't think she'd mind. It's not the place to ask in a hospice is it?

 NANA HAS ASKED DAVE TO TAKE HER HOME SO SHE CAN PICK UP MORE THINGS FROM ELSIE'S HOUSE

NANA: Oh David, David, there might be one or two things for Baby David's farmyard there. There's a couple of drawers I haven't had time to look in yet.

DAVE: **Did you get me them pipe cleaners Denise?**

DENISE: **Oh no, there weren't any.**

DAVE: Did you look?

DENISE: Yeah.

DAVE: Where?

DENISE: **Top Shop and Miss Selfridge.**

DAVE: Bloody 'ell!

DAD: Hey Sherlock Holmes, what do you want pipe cleaners for? You er smokin' the old pipe?

DAVE: No, I'm not smokin' a pipe, it's for Baby David's farmyard, you know, for the pigs' tails.

MAM: Oh Dave. I thought you weren't having any pigs

DAVE: Well they were hens originally Barbara but I put too much clay on them you know.

MAM: Oh Dave.

 EMMERDALE COMES ON THE TV. NANA VISIBLY CHEERS UP AND SETTLES IN TO WATCH. EVERYBODY HUMS ALONG TO THE THEME MUSIC. AS SOON AS IT FINISHES, JIM SWITCHES OVER TO ANOTHER CHANNEL

NAN: Oh Jim! That were Elsie rest in peace's favourite.

DAD: Well she can't bloody see it now, can she?

MAM: Jim!

DAD: Well that's all we've had all bloody afternoon. Elsie, Elsie, Elsie rest in bloody peaces. I've heard more about Elsie today than when the poor cow was alive.

MAM: Jim!

DAD: Well bloody 'ell, come on, she's dead and buried now.

MAM: Cremated!

DAD: Well dead and bloody cremated.

DENISE: Dad! Elsie was Nana's best friend.

DAD: **Best friend my arse.**

MAM: Jim I don't believe you sometimes. You've got no sympathy in you at all.

DAD: Well all she did when she was alive was bloody slag her.

NANA: I've never slagged Elsie.

DAD: Go way! Remember that time you slagged her something bloody rotten because she forgot your birthday.

NANA: **I never forgot hers.** PAUSE **She never did him any harm.**

MAM: **No.**

NANA: He's happy to eat her bacon.

MAM: Yeah. Jim! Just drop it now.

JIM: Elsie this, Elsie that. She's just angling to move in here. I tell you what, I bet you were bloody delighted when Elsie bloody croaked.

A LONG STUNNED PAUSE

CHERYL: Antony's been a long time at the chippy.

NANA: I can't believe it. It never crossed my mind that I might move in here. Although I'm the only elderly lady living in the flats and you've got a spare room here. It never crossed my mind Barbara. It didn't Barbara.

MAM: No. Denise get your Nana another brandy.

NANA: Oh ta love.

DENISE: **Cheryl, can you get Nana a brandy.**

CHERYL: Yeah.

DAD: You may as well bring the bloody bottle, Cheryl. She's supped Elsie out of house and home she may as well start on us.

NANA: May God forgive you Jim Royle for speaking ill of the dead like that.

DAD: I wasn't speaking ill of the dead. I was speaking about you, the living bloody dead.

LIVING ROOM.

EVERYONE IS STILL WAITING FOR THEIR CHIPS.

DAD: Dave after them chips, d'you fancy a quick medicinal drink down at the Feathers?

MAM: You're not having a quick one tonight Jim, you had a drink last night.

DAD: **Sod this, I'm off for a chat with the Arabs.**

CHERYL: What d'you mean Jim?

DAD: Mustapha Crap! Mustapha Crap!

MAM: Oh Jim!

DAVE: Yeah, good one James.

JIM LEAVES THE ROOM

DENISE: Nana take no notice of him.

NANA: Oh I don't love. It's in one ear and out the other. He doesn't respect the dead, Denise. That's the trouble.

MAM: He does really Mam. Take no notice.

A LONG PAUSE. THEY ALL WATCH TV

DAD: OOV OUT OF BABY MONITOR – JIM DOES ELSIE'S GHOSTLY VOICE
Wooooooo. Woooooo. Is anybody there? It's Elsie may I rest in peaces here. Wooooo. Call yourself a friend Norma. Leave my stuff alone you robbin' old get! EVERYBODY ROARS WITH LAUGHTER

Episode 5

 LIVING ROOM. JIM, BARBARA, DENISE AND DAVE. ANTONY HAS JUST TAKEN BABY DAVID UP TO BED. BARBARA HANDS DENISE A CIGARETTE

DENISE: **Ah ta Mam.**

THEY ARE ALL WATCHING SHOPPING CITY

MAM: **Oh Dave, how's the farmyard going?**

DAVE: Oh it's all right Barbara. I've nearly finished it now. I want to give it to Baby David next week on the morning of his christening as a present you know.

DAD: D'you want any er bullshit for it Dave, only I think Barbara's got plenty of it going spare.

JIM LAUGHS AT HIS OWN JOKE.

DENISE: Oh Mam guess what right. The other day right, I just took me eyes off Baby David just for a second right, while Richard and Judy was on, and the next thing he only tipped a full ashtray all over himself.

MAM: Aah. Aren't they lovely at that age? Aah I bet he looked dead cute, didn't he?

DENISE: Yeah. I didn't have the heart to tell him off 'cause, you know, they're into everything at that age aren't they?

MAM: Yeah.

DENISE: Dave took a picture of it.

MAM: Oh, was Dave there?

DENISE: No but I waited 'til he came home from work you know.

DAVE: It's a belter, Barbara.

MAM: Aah.

 LIVING ROOM. ANTONY IS PEELING POTATOES

MAM: Antony, tell everybody about you going to London next week.

ANTONY: Oh yeah, um, yeah, me and Darren's going to London next week.

DAVE: London!

ANTONY: Yeah.

DENISE: London!

ANTONY: Yeah.

DAD: Bloody London!

ANTONY: Yeah.

DAD: What's that about then Lurchie?

ANTONY: Well we've decided to reform 'cause Darren thought of a really good riff.

DAD: Oh that's bloody good news. It's nice to know that you're not living in a dream world wasting your time.

MAM: Oh Jim, leave him alone. Why can't you ever encourage him? Antony, I think it's great what you're doing love.

DAD: So have you had any er, any appointments or that down there Lurchie?

ANTONY: No. We're just gonna go in and let the tape speak for itself you know.

DAD: So you know like where the old record companies 'n' that are down in London do you?

ANTONY: **Not really, no.**

DAD: Well you're not just going to wander the streets of London hoping to bump into the head of E M bloody I, are you? Bloody hell. Come on, son

MAM: **Our Antony reminds me of um...**

DENISE: Who?

MAM: Oh him. What's his name? **Dick Whittington.**

DENISE: Ah yeah.

DAD: Oh aye, he's like Dick Whittington without the bloody Whittington.

EVERYBODY LAUGHS EXCEPT ANTONY.

 STILL TALKING ABOUT LONDON...

DENISE: **Hey Antony, is Emma going with you to London?**

ANTONY: **No.**

DENISE: **Why not?**

ANTONY: **Well you know it's a business trip, in't it?**

EVERYBODY LOOKS AT EACH OTHER AMAZED AT THE CONCEPT OF ANTONY HAVING A BUSINESS INTEREST.

MAM: **Business trip. Oh Antony, I'll have to do you some sandwiches.**

DAD: **Oh aye, you can share them out in the boardroom.**

ANTONY: **Hey, you having this Dave ey?**

ANTONY JUGGLES THE POTATOES.

DENISE: **Hey!**

MAM: **Oooh! Ohhh he's always been gifted with his hands.**

DAVE: **Good lad, budly.**

DENISE: **Oh Dave, show me mam what you can do with your finger, that trick.**

DAVE SHOWS THEM A SAD TRICK WITH HIS FINGER.

DENISE: **Yeah.**

HE DOES IT AGAIN.

MAM/
DENISE: **Ohhh.**

MAM: **Aah. How long have you been able to do that, Dave?**

DAVE: **Umm, I think it was about, yeah, last March or April, summit like that. About last March or April wasn't it, Denise?**

DENISE: **I think it was about last March. Or April. Something like that.**

MAM: **How did you find out you could do that, Dave?**

DAVE: **Well, I was in the doctor's surgery, and they had no magazines you know. So I was just messing about going like that** HE FLICKS HIS FINGER **and then suddenly it just went to that.**

DAVE DOES IT AGAIN. DENISE AND BARBARA ARE FASCINATED

MAM: Oh it's great that Dave, in't it great, Deni

DENISE: Yeah.

DAVE: It just went to that.

DAVE DOES IT AGAIN.

DENISE: He's always been great doing anything like that Dave.

MAM: Aah.

DAD: I tell you what, Dave, I better book the bloody Palladium for you two, hadn't I? Bloody 'ell, it's no wonder Bruce Forsyth keeps on bloody working.

THEY ALL LAUGH. JIM TRIES TO DO DAVE'S FINGER TRICK HIMSELF DISCREETLY. HE STOPS WHEN BARBARA CATCHES HIM. EVERYBODY LAUGHS.

NANA HAS COME DOWNSTAIRS FROM THE BATHROOM.

NANA: Oh Barbara, I think I might go upstaris and have another try. I can feel some movement. What d'you think, Barbara?

MAM: Yeah.

DAD: Bloody hell fire.

MAM: What's up with you?

DAD: Well I was gonna go. I've been baking one since she was up there the last time, I can't bake it much bloody longer.

DENISE: Dad!

MAM: Jim!

DAD: # I've been looking forward to this shite.

DENISE: Dad, you could have kept that to yourself thank you very much.

DAD: ## Not for much bloody longer I couldn't.

NANA: RESIGNED Barbara, let him go on the toilet if he wants to.

MAM: **No, Mam, you go on the toilet. Jim can wait.**

DAD: Barbara, let her go on the toilet.

NANA: Barbara, let him go on the toilet.

DAD: Barbara, let her go on the toilet.

NANA: Barbara, let him go on the toilet.

DAD: # Let her go on the toilet.

MAM: **Jim, all this toilet talk, we're about to start eating our tea.**

DAD: Well it's probably a bloody false alarm with her anyway like it was the last time. Anyway, I was gonna deal with that furniture while I was up there.

MAM: **What do you mean?**

DAD: # Doing a couple of stools.

Episode 6

 JIM, BARBARA, DAVE, DENISE, BABY DAVID, ANTONY, NANA, EMMA, DARREN, MARY, JOE, CHERYL, TWIGGY AND MICHELLE ALL PILE INTO THE LIVING ROOM.

THEY ARE DOING THE CONGA. EVERYONE HAS BEEN TO THE FEATHERS AFTER BABY DAVID'S CHRISTENING. PJ WHO IS GAUNT, UNSHAVEN AND WEARING A LARGE OLD-FASHIONED HEARING AID SLOWLY FOLLOWS THEM IN

DAD: **Come in. Come in to my modest little home. Sit yourselves down. Come on now everybody, make yourselves at home. Sit yourselves down now. Come on everybody. Find yourselves a chair.**

THE CAMERA MOVES IN TO THE KITCHEN WHERE BARBARA, NANA, MARY, DENISE AND CHERYL ARE TALKING

MAM: **Oh Denise, Denise what was that other little baby called that was being christened.**

DENISE: **Oh em, Brittney.**

MAM: **Weren't that other family dead rough?**

ALL: **Oh yeah.**

NANA: **That were a lovely service though Barbara. I do like that man that did it, that Vicar. He was great at Elsie's funeral you know.**

MAM: That wasn't him, Mam. The Vicar at Elsie's funeral was Jamaican.

NANA: **Oh was he.** SHE HOOTS WITH LAUGHTER

MAM: **Oh Denise, wasn't Baby David lovely when they put the water on his head?**

ALL: Yeah.

DENISE: **Ah yeah, and he didn't cry or nothing did he?**

ALL: No.

DENISE: Dave did though, he cried buckets. PAUSE Ah ey, Mam?

MAM: What?

DENISE: **What d'you think of Twiggy's new girlfriend?**

MAM: Oh well yeah, she seems alright. It's nice to see him happy though in't it?

DENISE: Yeah.

NANA: **Well I don't like her.**

MAM: Mam!

NANA: I DON'T LIKE HER. I'VE SEEN PLENTY OF HER TYPE ROUND THE FLATS.

KITCHEN. MARY, BARBARA, DENISE.

MARY: **Oh Barbara, I haven't told you have I?**

MAM: Oh what Mary?

MARY: Cheryl went to see a clairvoyant in the precinct yesterday and she told her that she'd find love in either two days, two weeks, two months or two years. Isn't that marvellous?

DENISE/
MAM: Aah yeah.

MAM: Oh Mary that's wonderful news.

MARY: **It is isn't it.**

LIVING ROOM.

JIM HAS JUST FINISHED TELLING A JOKE. EVERYONE LAUGHS.
MICHELLE LAUGHS LOUDEST AND LONGEST

MICHELLE: **Hey tricky bollocks, never mind your jokes pass us one of them lagers**

JIM PASSES HER A CAN

MICHELLE: **Hair of the dog this. I tell you what I'm gonna get absolutely rat-arsed today.**

SHE OPENS HER CAN

DAD: **So am I kiddo. Tell you what Twiggy, she's a girl after me own heart, her.**

MICHELLE: **Have you got any whisky here, Jim?**

DAD: **No, but feel free to go to the offy and buy one.**

MICHELLE: **Kiss me arse.**

THEY ALL BURST OUT LAUGHING.

DAD: **Did you two, eh, did you go out last night, Twig?**

TWIGGY: **Yeah, we went out for a few ales and then a ruby. Hey there was a bit of a to do with Farook and some lads who didn't want to pay the bill.**

DAD: **Go way.**

TWIGGY: **Yeah, anyway Michelle steamed in and sorted them out. Farook gave us free nans and pompadoms, didn't he Mich?**

MICHELLE: **Yeah, but I tell you what, I asked that Farook for extra chillis, but this morning. Ohhh. Talking of which, I think I need the shit house now.**

MICHELLE LEAVES AND GOES TO THE KITCHEN.

DAD: Ooh, tell you what lad, you've got yourself a bit of class there, haven't you?

TWIGGY: I tell ya, she don't half play a good tune on the old flute as well.

 KITCHEN. DENISE, BARBARA, MARY AND MICHELLE. CHERYL COMES IN.

MAM: Ahh Cheryl congratulations.

DENISE: I'm dead, dead, dead pleased for you.

CHERYL: Thanks everyone.

MICHELLE: What's all this about?

MAM: Ah well, Cheryl went to see a clairvoyant yesterday and she said she'd find true love in two days, two weeks, two months or two years.

MICHELLE: Who told you this, Cheryl?

CHERYL: Gemini Astrid, up the precinct.

MICHELLE: Gemini Astrid?

CHERYL: Yeah.

MICHELLE: For three quid?

CHERYL: Yeah.

MICHELLE: She talks complete bollocks she does love, I'd take no notice.

MAM: Oh Cheryl. You'd found love and now you've lost it.

MARY: Better to have loved and lost than never to have loved at all.

MAM: Yeah.

CHERYL: Yeah.

BIG PAUSE

MAM: **Cheryl, do you want a sausage roll?**

CHERYL: **Yeah I will thanks, Barbara.**

 # MARY WALKS IN TO LIVING ROOM WITH MORE FOOD.

DAVE: Y'alright.

MARY: Fine thank you, fine thanks Dave. PAUSE Oh Dave I do love the farmyard you made for Baby David.

DAVE: Do you Mary?

MARY: Oh I do Dave, I do. It's beautiful. It reminds me of being back home in Ireland.

MARY GOES BACK TO THE KITCHEN

DAVE: Does anyone else want to come and see Baby David's Farmyard?

DAD: Where is it Dave?

DAVE: **It's in the back of me van.**

DAD: Oh you make sure you keep the bloody back doors shut. We don't want them sheep getting out all over the bloody road, do we Joe.

EVERYONE LAUGHS

DAD: ASIDE TO TWIGGY **Bloody 'ell all this fuss over a bloody farmyard. Everyday it's farmyard this and farmyard that. It's only an old piece of plywood with balls of cotton wool stuck on the bugger. Sheep my arse. Anyway I'm off to shake out the one eyed milkman. Wayhey!**

DAVE AND DENISE ARE IN THE BEDROOM LEANING OVER BABY DAVID.

DAVE: And it took two of us to lift the fridge freezer out. Then we stopped for dinner and I had chips, peas and pudding.

DENISE: **Hey Dave, what you doing?**

DAVE: Just talking to Baby David.

DENISE: I never know what to talk to him about.

DAVE: Well I talk to him about work, you know, removals wise.

DENISE: **Well what can I talk to him about?**

DAVE: Well you could talk to him about Trisha, or Kilroy or Richard and Judy.

DENISE: **Or Esther.**

DAVE: Or Esther.

DENISE: **Or Ricki Lake.**

DAVE: Or Ricki Lake. See you've got loads to talk to him about.

DENISE: Yeah.

CUT BACK TO THE FRONT ROOM

DAD: **Come on Barb. Our party piece.**

BARBARA RUNS INTO THE FRONT ROOM FROM THE KITCHEN AND THEY BEGIN TO SING 'I KNOW THAT SOME DAY YOU'LL WANT ME TO WANT YOU'. EVERYONE JOINS IN AND DANCES AROUND THE ROOM. CUT BACK TO THE BEDROOM WHERE DENISE AND DAVE ARE STILL TALKING OVER BABY DAVID.

DAVE: He loves this song.

DAVE PUTS ON A TAPE OF RADIOHEAD ON BABY DAVID'S CASSETTE PLAYER AND DENISE AND DAVE HUM ALONG NEXT TO IT **See you are a good mother.**

MAM: OOV **Denise! Dave! Oh come down, our Antony's got an important announcement.**

DENISE: **Oh.**

DENISE AND DAVE GO DOWNSTAIRS. CUT TO FRONT ROOM WHERE EVERYONE IS SINGING THE LAST FEW BARS OF 'NEW YORK NEW YORK' AND REALLY GOING FOR IT. THE MUSIC IS CUT SHORT

MAM: **Sssh Sssh everbody 'cause our Antony's got a little announcement to make**

A LOT OF SSHHHING AND 'QUIETS' AS THINGS SETTLE DOWN.

DAD: **Oh it's not a job offer is it Lurchie?**

MAM: **Shut up Jim, let him say it.**

DAD: **Well go on Lurchie, get on with it.**

ANTONY: **Em, em, well em, me and Emma, em, we're getting engaged.**

A BIG CHEER AND LOTS OF OHS AND AHS FROM EVERYONE EXCEPT FROM JIM AND BARBARA. THE CHEERS DIE DOWN

MAM: `Not pregnant are you Emma?`

DAD: `Course she bloody is.`

Episode 7

LIVING ROOM.

JIM, DENISE, DARREN, DAVE, NANA. IT'S CHRISTMAS DAY. THE ROOM IS DECORATED FOR CHRISTMAS AND BABY DAVID'S FIRST BIRTHDAY. ANTONY AND DARREN HAVE JUST TAKEN BABY DAVID UP TO BED

JAM: **I'm gonna clear up later, Denise. Let's have a quick ciggy.**

DENISE: Yeah.

JAM: Here y'are.

DENISE: Oh ta.

JAM: Denise?

DENISE: Yeah.

JAM: **Do you think they'll want to sit down or stand up?**

DENISE: Well remember they are vegetarians, so they'll probably want to sit down.

JAM: Oh yeah. I've done tinned salmon and some hard boiled eggs, what else do they eat Denise?

DENISE: Well. Well you could make turkey sandwiches for everyone and then they can just take the turkey out themselves.

MAM: Oh yeah.

DAD: Why are you going to all that trouble for Barb? Bloody 'ell. They' re only popping in for ten bloody minutes aren't they?

MAM: **Jim, I'm only doing a finger buffet.**

DAD: **Finger my arse.**

MAM: **Oh!**

            EVERYONE LAUGHS

DAD: **Are you having that Dave, finger my arse!**

DAVE: **Good one that James.**

            THE DOORBELL GOES.
            EVERYONE IS VERY EXCITED.

DAD: **Lurch, come on son, answer the bloody door.**

            EMMA'S PARENTS ROGER AND VALERIE KAVANAGH ARRIVE. MANY 'HIYAS' LATER

MAM: **Oh well come on then, come and sit down. Come on everybody. Jim put some music on. Jim! Jim! Jim!**

            JIM FINALLY GETS UP

DAD: **All right Barb, bloody 'ell.**

NANA: Can I sit next to Valerie, Barbara?

MAM: Yes, yes, do you want to sit there Valerie. There, yeah. You sit there then Mam. Denise, will you help me with that?

ROGER GIVES JIM A MAGNUM OF CHAMPAGNE

ROGER: **There you go Jim.**

DAD: **Ooh lovely, bottle of Moet.** HANDS IT TO DAVE **There you go Dave.** QUIETLY **Hide that 'til the bugger's gone.**

NANA AND VALERIE ARE SITTING AT THE TABLE. BARBARA AND DENISE ARE IN THE KITCHEN TRYING ON VALERIE'S COAT IN THE BACKGROUND.

NANA: **I have a friend called Valerie.**

VALERIE: **Oh have you?**

NANA: **Sadly, she's been sectioned.**

PAUSE

NANA: **Your Roger's a big fat lad, in't he?**

VALERIE LAUGHS. DENISE COMES THROUGH FROM THE KITCHEN

DENISE: **Would you like a hard boiled egg, Valerie?**

VALERIE: **Oh thanks.**

VALERIE, NANA, MAM, DENISE ARE NOW SITTING ROUND THE DINING ROOM TABLE.

VALERIE: **Oh yes, I've gone from a B to a D Barbara.**

NANA: **What's she had done?**

DENISE: **Implants Nana.**

NANA: **Oh! Are you all right sitting in that hard back chair, Valerie?**

VALERIE: **Oh yes.**

NANA: Oh.

MAM: Oh they're lovely Valerie. Jim, don't Valerie's implants look lovely?

DAD: **Oh aye, they're great them, Valerie.**

DENISE: They're lovely, Valerie.

MAM: Dave?

DAVE: Umm.

MAM: Aren't they lovely?

DAVE: **Yeah, they're smashing them, er, two Valerie.**

MAM: Oh Valerie, Mary next door will be really sick she's missed them.

ROGER: I got her them for Christmas you know.

DAD: Oh well done.

ROGER: She didn't want 'em. **She wanted a Dyson.**

MAM: Oh well, I'd love a Dyson.

DENISE: I'd love a Dyson.

VALERIE: Well actually I did get a Dyson as well.

DENISE/
NANA/
MAM: **Ohhh.**

MAM: **Valerie, what a Christmas, implants and a Dyson.**

NANA: It was in the paper about a woman who had implants, and she went on an aircraft and her implants blew up the aircraft.

MAM: No they didn't blow up the plane, Mam. They just popped out of her bra

NANA: Valerie, Valerie, er, did they say anything about aircraft when they installed your implants.

VALERIE: No.

PAUSE

NANA: Barbara, didn't Elsie next door have implants?

MAM: No, eggplants Mam.

NANA: Oh.

DENISE: Em Valerie? Er I wanted to have a breast reduction but um Dave wouldn't let me.

MAM: Well he works very long hours Denise, be fair.

DENISE: Yeah.

MAM: You're lovely and slim Valerie. Isn't she Denise, lovely and slim?

DENISE: Oh yeah Valerie, you're lovely and slim Valerie.

VALERIE: Oh well Roger treated me to liposuction for me birthday, so I had me thighs and me tummy done.

MAM/
DENISE: Oh.

MAM: ## Liposuction. Oh I'd love liposuction.

DENISE: ## Oh yeah, I'd love liposuction.

NANA: ## So would I. What is it exactly Valerie?

VALERIE: Well, it's a technique where they suck out the fatty deposits in your body.

NANA: Oh, I was thinking of Cheryl next door. She could do with some liposuction, couldn't she?

DAD: She could always borrow Valerie's Dyson. You having that one David? Are you?

ROGER: **You ever been on a cruise, Jim?**

DAD: Um, oh no, no, no.

ROGER: We're going on a cruise this year.

DAVE WHISTLES.

DAD: Bloody 'ell.

MAM: **Are you Roger?**

ROGER: It takes in all the Med and then we come back and jump on the Orient Express.

NANA: Ooh!

ROGER: Have you ever been on the Orient Express Jim?

NANA: There's a lot of murders on the Orient Express, you want to watch it on that. In't that right Barbara?

MAM: What?

NANA: There's always murders on the Orient Express.

ROGER IS STILL GOING...

ROGER: Ey, I tell you what Jim, Valerie you can organise this. We'll get 'em all down on the boat. It's a forty-two footer you know.

DAVE WHISTLES.

DAVE: **Has it got a toilet?**

ROGER: **It's got two.**

DAVE WHISTLES AGAIN.

ROGER: There's the Jag Jim. See it. See the number plate ROG1.

DAVE WHISTLES.

DAD: Bloody lovely that, lad.

ROGER: It's just the run about really. I mean I've got a classic Aston Martin in the garage at home. It's just a bit of a toy really, but it's nice to have in't it?

DAD: **Too bloody true, that is lad. Yeah.**

ROGER: Do you know I stay at a lot of hotels you know when I'm away on various jobs. Do you know the first thing I do, Jim? (JIM SHAKES HIS HEAD.) I check in and then I pop upstairs and I check the old tug TV. You know what I mean.

DAD: Oh too right Roger, oh aye, yeah.

ROGER: You know where I was the other night. I went to one of them lap dancing clubs.

DAD: What are they like them?

ROGER: You pay a tenner and you see the lot.

DAD: A tenner?

ROGER: **Yeah, but you can't touch like.**

DAD: A tenner and you can't touch?

ROGER: No.

DAD: **Can you keep your hands in your pockets?**

GREAT BIG LAUGH FROM JIM AND ROGER

ROGER: I've got this woman I see in Hale right. She calls herself a stress manager. You know what I'm saying don't you.

DAD: Oh I do, I do.

ROGER: She specialises in Masons. She does all of us. Ohh Jim she knows some tricks. I tell you what she does things to me that Valerie couldn't even dream of.

DAD: Oh aye.

ROGER: And she lets me do things to her that you wouldn't even do to a farmyard animal.

DAD: Go on Rog, go on, you're havin' me on.

ROGER AND JIM ARE LAUGHING

DAVE: **Roger, I made a farmyard for Baby David.**

DAD: **Bloody 'ell Dave!**

 ## ROGER AND VALERIE HAVE LEFT. JIM STORMS UPSTAIRS AND GOES INTO SEE BABY DAVID.

DAD: MUMBLING AS HE ENTERS: **Yes Roger, no Roger** Shall I kiss you're **bloody arse Roger.** TO BABY DAVID Hey alright cock, alright ey, hey I wish I'd have bloody well stayed here with you instead of downstairs with big gob bloody Humpty Dumpty head Roger. Hey are you having this Baby David, he's got a bloody yacht, a bloody Aston bloody Martin, he's got a big bloody house in the country, he's got a box at Man United a box at bloody Manchester City. Hey and he's got a lovely tart out in Hale. And what have I got? I've got absolutely bloody nothing. We haven't even got a bloody Dyson. Hey and no one would have loved to have got a pair of bloody implants for Barbara more than me, ooh and I'd have got so much enjoyment out of them. But what have I got? I've got absolutely bloody nothing. Nothing – I never have had. I haven't go two ha'pennies to rub together. I'm always bloody skint and I always will be. Where did it all go wrong Baby David?

FRONT ROOM. ANTONY, DENISE, NANA, DAVE AND BARBARA.

DENISE: Hey Mam, does Dad still think we haven't got him a present this year?

MAM: Yeah.

JIM COMES BACK INTO THE ROOM AND SITS IN HIS CHAIR

DENISE: Dad?

DAD: Um.

DENISE: Aren't you bothered that we didn't get you anything this year?

DAD: LAUGHS Why change the habit of a lifetime?

DENISE: Well, we all clubbed together, even Nana, and er we got you this.

SHE HANDS HIM AN ENVELOPE AND JIM READS OUT WHAT IS WRITTEN ON IT.

DAD: To the best dad and husband in the world. From your loving family.

JIM OPENS THE ENVELOPE

Dad: Sky! Sky TV! You've got me Sky TV. 200 channels!

CUT

Roger my arse!!